My Soul Whispered
'ENOUGH'

Collapse, Courage & Coming Home

LORRAINE TRAVIS

ABOUT THE AUTHOR

Lorraine Travis writes from the place where collapse meets clarity, and something truer begins.

Lorraine spent decades holding it all together, as a mother, wife, and senior human resources professional, before her soul finally whispered, "enough." At forty, she chose meaning over convention. At sixty, she faced a deeper truth: despite all the progress she had made, she was still giving herself away to roles, identities, and the unrelenting cost of keeping up.

My Soul Whispered Enough is Lorraine's debut memoir: a candid, courageous story of burnout, awakening, and beginning again with clarity and heart. It is not written from the pedestal of resolution, but from the trenches of transformation.

Lorraine is the founder of LIFEWork Harmony™, an employment operating model that reimagines how people and work can thrive together. Her forthcoming book, *Aligned*, builds on this vision by exploring how to live and work in true alignment, without losing yourself in the process.

Known and loved by her husband since she was fifteen, Lorraine finds her deepest grounding in the love of their children and grandchildren, and in the rhythm of the ocean, her lifelong sanctuary.

Copyright © Lorraine Travis 2025
First published by Hembury Books in 2025
hemburybooks.com.au
info@hemburybooks.com
ISBN [9781923517370] (paperback)
ISBN [9781923517363] (ebook)
The moral right of the author has been asserted.
All rights reserved. No portion of this book may be reproduced in any form without permission from the author and publisher, except as permitted by Australian copyright law.

 A catalogue record for this book is available from the National Library of Australia

DEDICATION

To the silence that taught me how to hear.

CONTENTS

PREFACE	XI
An invitation to walk with me	XI
CHAPTER 1 | WHEN SILENCE SPEAKS	1
The first thread	1
Quiet beginnings	3
Unsettled	5
The Nativity and Christmas Eve	10
CHAPTER 2 | THE ECHOES OF SILENCE	13
In the hands that built us	13
Afternoons at the convent	15
CHAPTER 3 | THE COST OF OBEDIENCE	18
Opposing truths: a father and daughter	18
The cost of belonging	24
CHAPTER 4 | LEGACY	28
The shape of silence	28
The Inheritance	35
The soldiers of silence	38
Reflection of the grown child	39

CHAPTER 5 | LOVE ON A LEASH — 41

The perfect man — 41
The proposal — 43
Love without conditions — 44
The pregnancy and the push — 45
The ring and the motorbike — 46
The wedding that planned itself — 49
The difference between choice and promises kept — 52

CHAPTER 6 | WHEN SURVIVAL ISN'T LIVING — 54

The silent terms of welcome — 54
The difference of choice and promises kept — 57

CHAPTER 7 | FRACTURED STILLNESS — 67

The still years — 67

CHAPTER 8 | THE BUSINESS OF ME — 75

The ordinary that was everything — 75
The ache of more — 76
Back to work — 79
Where I gave myself away — 82
My body had other plans — 84

CHAPTER 9 | THE SILENT COLLISION — 88
The garage, the Jeep and the bond — 88
Ocean whispers — 90

CHAPTER 10 | LESSONS IN SILENCE — 92
The turn towards HR — 92
Navigating friendship and hierarchy — 93
Learning the unspoken rules — 94
Taking initiative — 94
Doing the work anyway — 95
The illusion of opportunity — 96
Misjudged by the role — 96
No title no voice — 97
Redefined by others, reclaimed by self — 98

CHAPTER 11 | THE RECKONING — 99
Thrown in without a net — 99
Trial by fire — 100
Creating the solution — 101
Where it turned — 102
The choice — 102

CHAPTER 12 | THE RETURN — 104
A just exit — 104
The gift of hard lessons — 105
Integrity as a compass — 107

CHAPTER 13 | THE MOUNTAIN AND THE LANDSLIDE — 109
The measure of a leader — 109
Unseen, unheard, undone — 111

CHAPTER 14 | THE QUIET RETURN — 117
Not starting over; starting differently — 117
Work as a mirror — 118
The power of not explaining — 118
The kind of leader I became — 118
What I no longer carry — 119
Reclaiming the self — 119
The strength in quiet resolve — 119

PROLOGUE
The beginning of alignment — 121

PREFACE

AN INVITATION TO WALK WITH ME

Come walk with me. Not as a stranger, but as someone willing to listen, to feel what's often forgotten, and to remember what it means to be fully human.

Life speaks softly at first, then louder when we forget to listen. This book isn't about the noise; it's about the whisper that remained when everything else fell silent.

I have lived a life made of moments, some rough-edged, some radiant, all real. There were times when love was fierce, when laughter echoed through rooms now quiet, when the smallest gesture spoke louder than a thousand words. And there were other times when silence sat heavily, and questions had no home. Each of those moments shaped me – grace, patience and the courage to begin again.

We often tell stories as if they have clear beginnings and tidy endings. Life isn't like that. My story is a circle, one that widens with each step. It began long before I was born, shaped by the generations who walked before me, and it continues with the choices I've made. Every person who crossed my path left a footprint. Some were gentle. Others, deep. All led me closer to understanding.

This isn't about reliving my past. It's about standing beside me as we trace the threads that weave a life. Not a perfect one; a real one. You'll meet a young girl learning what love means, a woman discovering her strength, a mother redefining home, and a soul learning to listen again. There will be laughter, mistakes and quiet revelations. Moments where you may see yourself reflected and pause, hearing your own whisper waiting to be heard.

Communication has always been my bridge between worlds, the way I reach across the distance between hearts. Words can wound. They can also heal. They help us understand what can't always be seen. When used with care, words aren't decoration; they're connection. That's why I write. And that's why I invite you to walk with me now.

As you read, I ask only this: listen not only to the story, but also to the silence between the sentences. Feel the rhythm of ordinary days, the weight of choices, the lightness of forgiveness. Let these pages remind you that life is not a test to pass, it is a conversation to live.

Every chapter that follows is a step on the path. Sometimes smooth, sometimes steep, always honest. I will not hide the shadows. They have taught me as much as the light. I will not dwell in sorrow either. There is beauty in truth, even when it is raw. And there is joy in remembering that survival is not the end of the story. It is where living truly begins.

So, take my hand. Let us walk slowly, with curiosity and compassion. Let us find the rhythm between words and silence, between the world as it was and the world as it might be. This is not my journey alone. It is a quiet exploration of what it means to belong, to forgive, to love, and to begin again.

The path is open. The whisper is waiting. Walk with me now.

CHAPTER 1

WHEN SILENCE SPEAKS

THE FIRST THREAD

On Thursday 26 February 1959, my father and grandfather Nunnu finalised the purchase of a small continental delicatessen on William Street in Darlinghurst. They were to open the doors the following day. That evening, however, life had other plans. My mother went into labour, unexpected and unplanned, and a new baby was on the way.

I have come to understand the era I was born into, when hospitals ran like military outposts and the air smelled of antiseptic and starch. Birth was a clinical procedure, not a shared experience. The emotional needs of parents were not considered. Labour was treated as part of a system; efficient and impersonal. It was an exclusive club for women, where pain was endured quietly and presence was measured by compliance, not connection.

Fathers waited in a room called the Stork Club, pacing the linoleum floors, flipping through outdated magazines, the scent of instant coffee lingering in the air. They were summoned only when the baby was swaddled and the mother propped up in bed, ready to be presented.

I was born around ten in the morning. While Mum laboured, Dad was at the shop arranging shelves, greeting customers, stepping into a new chapter of his life. The deli was small, narrow, and full of life. Wooden shelves lined the walls, stacked with tins of olive oil, jars of pickled vegetables and wheels of cheese wrapped in paper. Strings of salami and prosciutto hung behind the counter. The air carried a mix of sawdust, vinegar and coffee, sharp and comforting all at once.

Darlinghurst in those years was a neighbourhood of new beginnings. Maltese, Greek, Italian and Polish families had settled nearby, their accents mingling with those of the Australians who had lived there for generations. People came through the door curious and hungry – some were looking for the flavours of home, others were discovering them for the first time. The rhythm of conversation flowed between languages, punctuated by the hum of the fridge and the soft static of the ABC on the radio behind the counter.

In one corner of the shop there was a small sandwich bar, where fresh rolls were filled to order and customers stopped in for a quick bite. At first, the pie warmer held the usual favourites – meat pies, sausage rolls and Cornish pasties, the staples of every Australian lunch counter. Over time, things began to shift. My grandmother, Nanna, started baking her own pies, a Maltese version of Pastizzi known as a torta. She made the flaky pastry from scratch, resting it overnight so it was ready for rolling the next morning. Each day, trays of golden *torta* filled the air with the scent of butter and pepper, peas and ricotta, the aroma drifting out through the open door onto William Street. One by one, the meat pies, sausage rolls and Cornish pasties disappeared from the warmer, replaced by Nanna's creations. People stopped asking for the usual pies. They wanted hers instead. The *torta* became so popular that, in the end, they stopped selling the traditional meat pies altogether.

Dad was there among it all, serving customers, rearranging displays, learning how to make the business his own. The shop was more than a livelihood; it was a mark of identity, a promise of stability in a country still learning to embrace the cultures it had invited in.

There was no grand announcement, no glorious moment in which he was handed his newborn daughter. When he finally went home that evening, visiting hours had likely ended. They would not have let him in.

Years later, I asked Mum if he came to the hospital. She paused, then said she couldn't remember. That silence spoke volumes. If he had come, she would have remembered. There was a sharp sting in that realisation. I kept circling the question. Why would he have stayed away? It was simple. He was busy. He had responsibilities. He was building a future for his family.

Mum later told me that Dad had been busy in the shop. When he finished each day, it was already late, long after closing time. The shop was new to them, there were changes to make, stock to arrange, and their mark to leave. When the hospital finally called him to say Mum was being discharged, ten days after I was born, Dad went to collect her and take her home.

That was my first meeting with Dad. A quiet introduction, not at the moment of birth, but rather in the rhythm of his work.

QUIET BEGINNINGS

I remember going to the shop as a child. Dad was always working late. It was dark when we left for home, the streetlights already on. We would walk past the glowing shopfronts, the hum of the fridges still audible through the glass.

We walked on, past it all, until we reached the cul-de-sac at the end of the street and the huge sandstone wall that marked the turn. There, parked in its usual spot, was Dad's green Zephyr, the bonnet adorned with a gleaming silver plane, pointed and proud.

That car still evokes happy memories. It was a time when life felt good. Everyone seemed content, the world unfolding around us with a kind of ease that did not need to be named. I remember a trip to Melbourne. We went with our aunty and uncle, travelling in two cars. Dad's green Zephyr, which everyone affectionately called the big bag of wind, and our cousins' Simca, known as fondly as the teapot.

Dad had fitted a fold-up mattress in the back of the station wagon so my sister and I could sleep on the drive. We stopped at Mobil service stations along the way. They were running a promotion and gave out polystyrene planes to children. My sister and I each got one. We were thrilled. We played with them for days.

In Melbourne, I remember running around a park, a place I only came to know later as the Tan. Wind in our hair, our voices carrying across the grass. We had driven all that way to see Johnnie Catania, a Maltese singer. It felt like an adventure. Simple, joyful, unhurried. The kind of memory that settles softly in the chest and stays.

As a child, I never questioned the dynamic. Dad was always working. That was the rhythm of our lives. He was not the kind of father to sit on the floor, to play, to read bedtime stories. His presence was different. It was in the meals on the table, in the order he maintained at home, in the quiet pride of the shop.

There was love there. I know that now. Not the conventional sort. It was shaped through duty, not outward affection. Measured in hours, not in spoken words. And as a child, I learned to read between the lines. To take up as little space as possible. To notice the flicker behind a sigh.

My earliest years were not cradled in lullabies or lingering embraces. They were shaped through quiet observation.

Some of the deepest imprints are left by what we long for, not by what we receive.

Love, though imperfect and silent, can still shape us. Perhaps most importantly, I now understand that even when nothing is said, it can still be real.

Silence carries its own truths. Sometimes it takes a lifetime to learn to hear them.

I remember the bell above the door, the smell of salami and sawdust, the way he looked up from behind the counter, tired, smiling. That was his way of showing up.

CHAPTER 1

He never changed. When his last daughter was born, he stayed home again. The hospital rules had not changed. Neither had he. I do not remember being taken to the hospital to see Mum. No fuss was made about the new arrival. The last of five children: two girls, one boy, then another two girls. Dad had his son. The name would continue.

UNSETTLED

Mum said the birth was easy. That is where easy stopped. I cried constantly. Not the soft, whimpering cry of a restless baby. These were piercing, relentless wails. It was as if, even then, I already knew the world was not quite ready to hold me.

'She would not settle,' Mum once told a neighbour, her voice low, almost apologetic. 'Even when she was fed and dry. It was like she was ... searching.'

She told me every photo of me as a baby showed me crying. Not one with a smile. Only red cheeks, clenched fists, eyes squeezed shut. Those photos never made it to the mantelpiece.

There is one photo that stays with me, though I must have been no more than two or three months old. Mum is holding me. Her figure is slender, her hair neat, wearing a pencil skirt that fits her as though it were tailored. She looks beautiful. Composed. Young.

And there I am in her arms, crying with my whole body. My face scrunched in distress, as if the world itself were too much. She is looking at the camera, not at me.

I have always wondered what she was thinking in that moment. Whether she felt helpless, or simply resigned. There is no answer in her face. Only poise. Stillness. A kind of tired grace.

It is not a happy photo. It is honest.

That picture never made it to the mantelpiece either.

I was called a 'whining baby'. The kind that unsettled rooms and made people exchange glances. Looking back, I understand what she could not name. Two generations later, they have identified it: reflux. My son had it, and so did our grandson. They cried too, as I did. And in their cries, I finally heard the truth of my own beginning.

It must have been so hard for my mother, holding a child who could not be soothed. Always wondering if it was her fault. Or worse, if there was a fault in me. What she did not know, what no one knew then, was that it was a thread the generations had never fully understood.

It took science and medicine to recognise what mothers had been speaking of all along. It could not be ignored any longer. Like all good things, answers take time to emerge. Now that one exists, the problem has quietly disappeared. The thread has been broken.

Sometimes a thread can be broken not by force, but through understanding.

Answers are all around us. The things that shape us often come in the form of simple questions. Looking back now, I see that the whining baby was only doing what it knew to do – speaking with a voice that did not yet have words.

≈ ≈ ≈

I remember the bus ride from Mascot into Darlinghurst with Mum, the way the windows fogged up in winter. I would trace shapes with my finger on the glass. Mum's yellow dress with the lemon print. It was beautiful. I wanted one like it.

I always looked out the window because the building and the trees called out to me. The building still stands on the corner, proud. I still admire its beautiful architecture, and the same trees. I love them now the way I loved them then.

We would walk past the shop windows that glowed under the streetlights. Inside his deli, Dad moved behind the counter, quick and focused. I do not remember him slipping me treats or crouching to greet me. I remember being there, watching him work. That was our version of family time. Brief, practical, and always surrounded by the hum of effort.

CHAPTER 1

Was there love there? I would like to believe so. Through time and reflection, I've come to an understanding that, while it was not love in the traditional sense, it was something. It was shaped through duty, not affection. Measured in hours worked, not words spoken. And as a child, I learned to read between the lines. To find meaning in what was not said. It's only now, with distance and my own experience of parenting, that I can recognise the shape of it. Some of the deepest imprints are not left by what we are given. They are left by what we long for.

Love, though imperfect and unspoken, can still shape us. Perhaps most importantly, I've come to understand that silence carries its own truths. Even when nothing is said, it can still be real.

Lazy corner and cream buns

Back then, it was Lazy Corner.

That's what they called it, that small stretch on the corner of Coward Street and Botany Road in Mascot, near the GPO. A red garden bench, a strip of cracked footpath, and a circle of men who gathered like clockwork.

Every Saturday, it belonged to Nannu. I belonged to him. It belonged to me too.

He stood there with the other Maltese men, one foot resting on the bench, a hand in his pocket. They wore pressed trousers and leather shoes, even in the heat. Shirts tucked in, no matter what.

They spoke in Maltese, always. Fast, loud, sometimes overlapping. They didn't switch languages when children were near. They didn't slow down or explain.

They included us with a smile, a wink, a gesture to listen in. We were always close, running around, playing near the bench, circling the lamppost, hopping between the cracks in the footpath. And I understood them. Maybe not every word, yet 'ENOUGH'. *Enough* to laugh when they laughed. *Enough* to feel like I was part of it.

When I stood near Nannu, even with jam on my face and cream on my chin, I didn't feel like a tag-along.

I felt like I belonged.

He'd press a sixpence into my hand without looking at me.

'Go on then,' he'd say, not even pausing his sentence. 'Wilson's.'

Wilson's Cake Shop was down the street. I'd run there with a kind of quiet excitement, not jumping or skipping, moving fast 'ENOUGH' to show I belonged. The bell above the glass door rang as I pushed it open. Inside, the air was warm with sugar and vanilla.

I didn't browse. I already knew.

'One cream bun, please.'

The girl behind the counter would wrap it in waxed paper, twisting the top tight. I'd walk out holding it in two hands, the soft icing sugar sticking to my fingers. By the time I made it back to the bench, cream was already on my face, and jam had found its way to my chin.

Nannu never said anything. He'd glance at me, maybe raise one eyebrow, then keep talking. I always saw it, though – the corner of his mouth twitch, like he was trying not to smile.

The men would thin out as the morning wore on. When the conversations faded, Nannu would tap his thigh lightly and nod.

'Let's go.'

We took the long way home. Past L'Estrange Park, past the sandstone fence and the wide gum trees that dropped sticks and pods onto the pavement. Their bark peeled like old paper, and their leaves rattled in the breeze. He held my hand, loose and certain.

We didn't talk much. We didn't need to.

When we got back, the smell met us before the screen door did.

Not toast. Not cereal. Home mad couscous steaming over Minestrone soup. Garlic crackling in the frying pan and baked beans warming read to go over the couscous, yum.

The kitchen was the centre of the house, small, bright and alive. That table in the middle of the room was never clear. It was always full – mixing

CHAPTER 1

bowls covered with tea towels, trays of peeled potatoes, piles of herbs, pastry ready to be rolled out.

The radio didn't play. The house made its own noise. Cupboards opened and closed. Feet moved across the linoleum. Someone was always arriving, always calling out down the hallway.

Nanna moved between the stove and the table without fuss. Her apron was tied at the back, her hair pinned up. She didn't smile much while she worked. She was happy. She didn't need to perform it.

If she was making couscous, you could smell it. Not from a packet. In the sixties, you made it from scratch.

She would pour semolina into a large metal colander and set it over the pot of minestrone soup, which simmered below, thick and red, filled with beans and diced vegetables. As the steam rose, she would begin working butter into the semolina, her hands moving gently, rubbing and folding the grains as they softened. Not stirring. Working. It was a rhythm she knew in her bones.

Sometimes she folded a little couscous directly into the soup. Not always. Only when it felt right. I would sit at the table, legs swinging, and watch her ladle it into a bowl, the grains soft, the broth rich.

It was filling, and felt like being cared for.

Other days, she served the couscous as a plate of its own, golden and soft, and spooned over a sauce made with white butter beans, garlic, onions and tomato paste, cooked until the oil separated and the whole mixture turned a deep, beautiful red. She didn't say it was special. She placed the plate down in front of me.

And I ate it to my heart's content. The smell, the texture, the warmth. It was magic.

She made everything. Not only food. She made home.

Ravjul, lined up on floured trays, filled with fresh ricotta and served with her slow-cooked tomato sauce. She would grate parmigiana over the top with a metal grater that lived in the drawer. *Pastizzi*, filled and folded by hand. Spinach pies, cut into clean squares, golden at the edges. Roasts, with potatoes that soaked up all the flavour from the pan. Minestrone, always thick, never watery. And sometimes, when the milk was fresh, she would make *gbejniet*, homemade Maltese cheese.

She would heat the milk slowly, stir in junket, and wait. The curds rose gently. She scooped them into muslin, let them drain, and pressed them into soft, fresh cheese. She never served it cold. She served it warm, freshly made, the taste light and clean, nothing added.

We never called it special. It simply was.

Even now, the smell of onions in oil brings me back. The clatter of a spoon. The sound of the screen door closing behind someone.

She never said, 'I love you.' She didn't need to. Her love was cooked. Served. Ladled. Folded through couscous. Pressed into cheese. Held in every bite.

THE NATIVITY AND CHRISTMAS EVE

It always started with the buildings.

Nannu would clear two full corners of the lounge room, the same ones every year, and begin to build. Not with timber or tools, but with cardboard boxes he had collected from the shops. He would fold them flat, wrap them in brown paper, and bring them to life with chalk, pen and imagination.

He didn't simply stack boxes.

He built them.

There were houses, doorways, staircases, archways, rooftops. He constructed an entire street, with small hills and narrow lanes, each one shaped with care. Some boxes were stacked to make towers. Others were trimmed and bent to form walls and ledges. He used fabric to drape the hillsides, flour to mark dusted paths, and sand to line the road through the middle of the village.

It wasn't rushed.

It wasn't casual.

It was art.

CHAPTER 1

Then came the details, the ones that turned buildings into a world.

There was a marketplace, always, with tiny baskets and stalls set up like they were waiting for morning. There were gates, fences, low stone walls marked with pencil, and trees made from wire or twisted paper, standing in little patches of sand.

The stable came last. Low and open, built with strips of wood or cardboard, lined with straw. The crib sat at its centre, empty yet already sacred.

Once the village was built, he began to add the life.

And that was when the story started.

Nannu had so many figurines. More than I ever realised.

Not just the usual ones. There were Mary, Joseph, the baby Jesus, and a few animals, but there were also dozens more. Shepherds with sheep draped over their shoulders. Townspeople carrying baskets. Women kneeling. Men in robes. Children frozen mid-step. Angels. Goats. Camels. Chickens. Birds. Some looked like they came from other stories entirely, and still, they belonged.

He kept them carefully boxed, wrapped in tissue, packed away gently each year like a treasured collection. When he unwrapped them, it was like waking someone from sleep.

Each one had a place.

And Nannu knew exactly where that place was.

The three wise men never started at the stable. They began their journey far away, somewhere at the edge of the scene. Each day, he would move them a little closer. One step at a time. As if they were really travelling. By Christmas Eve, they were nearly there.

Never early.

And baby Jesus?

The crib stayed empty.

The straw was laid. The cloth was folded. The space was waiting. The baby didn't appear until after midnight. That was the rule. It didn't need to be spoken. We knew.

He never told us not to touch anything. He didn't have to.

There was a quality in the way he handled each piece. Slow. Quiet. Steady. It made you stop and watch. He would crouch low, close to the ground, his hand hovering before placing the figure. Then he would lean back slightly, eyeing the angle, adjusting if needed.

It wasn't decoration.

It was devotion.

And the Nativity did not simply sit in the room.

It became the room.

The fireplace stood between the two corners, and in front of it stood the Christmas tree. Tall. Sometimes real, sometimes artificial. Always dressed the same. Tinsel. Baubles. Handmade decorations. Ribbons tied by hand. The lights blinked slowly, casting a soft glow across the village. Shadows moved on the buildings like time passing.

There was no theme. No colour matching.

Only tradition.

Every year, we would come home late from church, every Christmas eve. Still in our good clothes, shoes kicked off at the door. The house would be quiet, and the lounge dim, lit only by the tree.

CHAPTER 2

THE ECHOES OF SILENCE

IN THE HANDS THAT BUILT US

I was seven when the tide began to shift. On weekends, Dad would drive us in circles through the suburbs, retracing the same streets. I did not know what he was seeking. Eventually, he found it. A block of land in Sydney's eastern suburbs. A new journey had begun.

Dad sold our old house, just down the road from the small white Anglican church where we occasionally attended Sunday school. Every Sunday morning, they rang the bell. I would lie in bed and listen to it, and feel sorry for the children who had to go.

That little white building became part of the rhythm of my mornings. When we moved, I missed the sound of the bell. And I missed the building too.

While our new home was being built, we moved in with our grandparents in Mascot. There were five of us: Mum, Dad, my older sister, my younger brother and me...

Our cousins lived two minutes away. We saw them nearly every day. After school, they came over until their parents finished work. We walked to school together, played together, visited each other's homes. We were a little pack.

We were not alone in starting again. Dad and his two sisters, with their families, all built houses in the same suburb. One was directly opposite ours. Another was around the corner. Three full families, complete with mothers, fathers and children, all within shouting distance. Thirteen children in total.

That closeness shaped a deeper bond. We were more than family. We were friends. Side by side, our lives intertwined. We built memories and shared adventures that have never faded. Though the years have scattered us, whenever we gather, we slip back into one another's company as if no time has passed.

During school holidays, we walked to the local pool and spent entire days there. Laughing. Splashing. Playing. By late afternoon, exhausted yet exhilarated, we wandered home. Sun-kissed and tired. Hair stiff with chlorine. Hearts full.

Most mornings, I rose early to attend church with Nannu. I treasured those quiet walks, the feel of his hand in mine, the scent of incense and old wood inside the church. Then we would return for breakfast, and he would accompany my sister, brother and me to school. In the afternoons, he waited to walk us home again. Nanna was always in the kitchen, making *torta*.

On Saturdays, Dad would haul us over to help at the new house. We gathered newspapers, stacked bricks, swept dust. It felt meaningful. We weren't just building a house, we were building a future. Afterwards, we explored caves, quarries, hills and hollows. A reservoir was being built nearby. To us, it was a playground. Freedom. Fun. Unstructured.

In winter 1967, we began moving into the new home: a red-brick, two-storey house that felt vast and strange. I remember sitting before the fire, warmth wrapping us like a blanket. On weekends we slept there, surrounded by boxes and the smell of fresh paint. Come Sunday, we would return to our grandparents' home to finish the school week. We completed the year at our old school, and by Christmas we moved in properly.

In 1968, we began at the new school. That year, Nannu died.

The night he passed is etched in memory. Dad received a call. His father's condition had worsened. He said he had had a vision and wished to see his family. Dad gathered us and drove us to the hospital. I recall standing around his bed in silence. Visitation hours had ended. Dad told us to kiss and hug him. I did not know we were saying goodbye.

Not long after we returned home, the phone rang again. Dad answered. His face changed. His father had died.

We knelt together in the lounge room and prayed the rosary for him. He had been a devout Catholic. It was what he did before he went to sleep each night, and that night the family said it one last time for him.

Dad was devastated. It was the first time I saw my father weep. That was his 'I love you.'

At his funeral, there was a mark of honour I have only ever witnessed on that day. As the hearse left the church, the attendant walked half a block, from the corner of Sutherland Street to the small grocery shop near L'Estrange Park, before continuing on to the cemetery. The funeral was a large procession. He was a big part of the community, loved by many.

AFTERNOONS AT THE CONVENT

The year was 1968. I was nine, my sister was ten, and my brother was seven. We had started at a new school and didn't know anyone in the area beyond our own family. Our cousins lived nearby, although they went to a different school. Both of our parents worked, and there were no childcare services available at that time. None. So Dad arranged for us to stay at the convent after school. It wasn't a choice; it was a necessity. The only option.

We had only recently moved out of Nanna and Nannu's home. Everything in our lives was changing quickly. A new house. A new school. New routines. Still, time at the convent moved slowly. It was quiet, strict and still.

The nuns were stern. Every afternoon they went to prayer, and we were expected to sit quietly, eat our sandwiches and wait. We were not to answer the door, not to move around, not to make noise. I didn't know that, not at first. One afternoon, the bell rang and I opened the door. I got a slap that left a welt. It was punishment for misbehaving, although I hadn't known the rule.

We sat outside to eat. The sandwiches were squashed, sometimes dry. What saved me was the view. The ocean. The convent sat above Lurline Bay, and from the front lawn you could see right out to the water. There was a small concrete bench, and that became my secret escape. I would swing my legs and stare out at the waves, letting the sea carry me somewhere else.

I never got caught. I did it every day. Sometimes I ate my sandwich. Sometimes I sat there, swinging my legs back and forth, watching the waves roll in and the sky shift above them. I never tired of it. That view was my comfort, my quiet retreat.

After our sandwiches, we were given a room to sit in. Now I realise it was probably a meeting room. We were told to do our homework and wait for Dad. When visitors came to the convent, we had to be silent. Still. Obedient.

What I remember most are not the rules. It is the small, quiet discomforts. The things we didn't say.

By the time we arrived each afternoon, our sandwiches were dry, curling at the edges. My youngest sister would hand hers to me and say, 'I don't want it.'

There were no warm greetings, no soft landings. Only dry sandwiches, silence and the sea. Yet in those afternoons, I began to learn a quiet and essential lesson. How to be still inside discomfort. How to listen, observe and wait. I didn't yet know that love could be quiet, that loss could leave a shape, or that belonging sometimes begins with not belonging at all.

≈ ≈ ≈

Whenever I reflect on who I am, I recognise that my understanding of love began in those quiet, precious moments with my grandparents. They were always present, fully in the moment, though I did not know it at the time. They offered their time without question. They treated all grandchildren equally. Each of us carries different stories, and still the feeling was shared – to be wanted, to be seen.

They built a foundation in me I still carry. A tradition of togetherness, a sense of belonging, a belief that love is shown, not merely spoken. Everything has a beginning, and it does not always begin with us.

Family lunches were held in the sunroom, the only room big enough to hold us all. The air was filled with the scent of roasted meats, fresh bread, *pudina* and laughter. Nannu's garden flourished in the backyard. A chicken coop, rows of fruit trees, peaches, plums and nectarines, fresh from the trees in their garden, and a bloom of flowers – hydrangeas, dahlias, carnations, camellias and frangipanis.

Those blooms still speak to me. When I see them now, I do not see petals alone. I see Nannu's hands in the soil, hear the rustle of leaves, feel the heft of his spade in my memory. I feel the warmth of family, grounded in earth. He did not need to speak much. His presence alone was enough.

In those early years, filled with absence and effort, quiet pride and crying babies, I began to learn a truth I would not be able to name until much later. That love is not always soft, or verbal, or obvious. Sometimes it is simply shown. In late nights behind a counter. In a sixpence pressed into a child's palm. In a silver plane gleaming on the bonnet of a parked car at the end of the day.

Sometimes, when no one can quite hear you yet, you learn to listen. Not only to others, but also to yourself.

CHAPTER 3

THE COST OF OBEDIENCE

OPPOSING TRUTHS: A FATHER AND DAUGHTER

Dad was an early riser: five-thirty, like clockwork.

Each morning, without a word, he would walk into our room and rip the blankets off from the bottom left-hand corner of my bed. It wasn't violent. It was definite, abrupt *enough* to send a clear message. The blanket came off, and that meant up and out.

He never said my name. I shared the room with my two sisters, and he didn't want to wake them. The routine was understood. I would get up, help him wash and dress, make his breakfast, and pack his lunch. I always added a piece of fruit. That was what we did. That was Dad.

The only thing I did for myself, the one small act of comfort, was laying my school uniform on the bed before I left the room, pulling the blankets back over it, and turning the electric blanket on. When I returned to get dressed, my clothes were warm.

CHAPTER 3

It was a small luxury I never spoke of. A quiet secret. In a life shaped by duty and routine, it was the only thing I did for me.

Dad needed help after he came home from the hospital. It was hard for him. He was in his early thirties and had lost his independence. Dad's mind and his tongue were still sharp. His body had changed, and his world had changed with it.

The doctors called him the miracle man. He had survived what many didn't. But survival came at a price. No medicine or technology could return what had been taken. His life had changed forever.

When I think about what Dad went through, from working, studying and succeeding to suddenly being told it was over, I imagine his life must have felt diminished. Yet every day, with quiet pride, he went to work.

Life changes. Dad had once run a busy shop with Nunnu, full of pride and purpose. Eventually, they sold it. A quiet ending to a chapter that had shaped so much of our early life.

Later, after the aneurism, everything changed again. He no longer had the capacity to return to mainstream work. He was capable. He wanted to contribute. But what took others ten minutes might take him twenty. That was what he was told, and over time, he came to believe it.

Instead, he made number plates and learned to weave beautiful cane baskets, strong and sturdy, like the version of him that remained.

With time and hindsight, I've come to understand the weight of what he carried after the aneurism. He was young, in his prime, and in an instant, everything was pulled out from under him. Work, routine, identity. Gone. How does anyone live with that? A young family, the pressure of survival, and the quiet feeling of being robbed. Where do you go with that kind of loss? Who do you turn to?

He never complained, not to us. The signs were there in the way he moved, in his anger and frustration. They all spoke of grief and shame. As a child, I didn't see it. I was busy living, and even later, I never gave it much thought

That was Dad. That was his normal. Now I understand. He was grieving, mourning the man he once was. I don't believe he ever truly got over it.

I can't begin to imagine the depth of his grief, or how alone he must have felt.

How could we have understood? We were children. All we saw was Dad, and that never changed.

Through his eyes, shaped by pain and quiet suffering, he believed we had ridiculed him, that we saw him differently. In truth, we had not. We were too young to ask questions, too unsure to offer comfort. We loved him, wholly and without condition. What became normal for us was a life he could never accept as his own.

Now, looking back on my own life, I know I'm only scratching the surface of his story. I will never fully understand what he carried or what he lost. Sometimes life is like that: sliding doors within the same house. People living side by side, each holding a different version of what's true, each believing their story is the only one. Two people, two truths, and somehow, the same love between them. That is life.

I've come to understand that my parents' silence was never about me. It wasn't personal; it was historical.

It began long before I was born, in what had been taken from them, in what they had endured, and in what they passed on without words.

And they were not the only ones.

The Wound That Wasn't Seen

It was that time of year again. Parent-teacher meetings. I remember the weight of the envelope in my schoolbag, the one the principal handed to me after class. She didn't say much. She placed it in my hand with a look that lingered a second too long. I knew it wasn't good news.

The letter asked my parents to call the school to arrange a suitable time to meet with the principal. It said there were concerns.

That evening, my parents called me into the room. My father was furious.

CHAPTER 3

'I've received a letter from the principal,' he snapped. 'She wants to see me, about you. What have you done?'

I started to talk. 'I don't know. I go to school every day, but...' Before I could finish, he cut me off.

'You're a liar,' he shouted. 'You know what you've done.'

He kept repeating himself, louder each time, and I kept crying, trying to explain through the tears.

'I don't know,' I said. 'I haven't done anything wrong. I haven't been in trouble.'

It didn't matter. Every word made it worse.

He hated that I was crying.

He shouted at me for saying 'I don't know' over and over, as if it were the worst thing I could say.

Then he stood up from his chair, and I knew what was coming. I didn't wait for it.

I took off out the back door, down the stairs and up the street towards the water reservoir.

That was my hiding place. Up there, I could disappear. The wind was sharp, the air cool, the ground uneven under my feet. It was quiet. I could breathe. I could cry without anyone hearing.

Our dog, Shiela, followed me. She didn't bark or fuss. She came.

She sat beside me while I cried, and I talked to her as if she understood. Maybe she did.

She stayed close, calm and still, as though she knew I needed her. She didn't ask for anything. She didn't interrupt. She listened.

I told her everything. That I tried. That I was tired. That I didn't want to be yelled at anymore. That I honestly didn't know what I had done wrong.

She didn't move. She didn't leave. She stayed. And that was *enough*.

I stayed there until the sky started to change, until the wind shifted and the air took on the feel of early evening. Then I got up, brushed the dirt off my clothes and went home. I slipped quietly through the back door, hoping not to be noticed.

As I passed my parents' room, I heard Mum on the phone. She was talking to her mother, my Nanna.

Her voice was low, strained, tired.

She was telling her about the appointment with the doctor and about Dad.

I caught fragments. The doctor had told him he had to be patient. I was too weary to take in the rest.

My head hurt. My ears rang. I remember thinking there was blood in my ear, though maybe it was only the heat from crying. I didn't stay to listen. I went straight to the bathroom, turned on the shower, and stood under the water until everything went quiet.

What I remember most are not the rules. It is the small, quiet discomforts. The things we didn't say.

≈ ≈ ≈

The next year, I received the Most Improved award. It still wasn't enough. He said I was lazy. That I wasn't trying. I was. I couldn't keep up.

Each morning, I cared for him until half past ten, when the driver came to take him to the sheltered workshop. Only then did I go to school. I was exhausted before the day had even begun. I wasn't failing from lack of care; I was barely awake *enough to* function.

The school eventually assigned me to the canteen. There were no mothers to run it. I left class before the bell, set up the counter, and served the other children. Morning tea. Lunchtime. Two sessions a day missed, on top of late arrivals.

They sent me for a psychiatric assessment. My parents took me to the city, dressed me in a new frock and shiny patent shoes. They squeaked when I walked, and I loved that sound.

For a moment, I thought I mattered.

CHAPTER 3

≈ ≈ ≈

One day, during the summer holidays, I cut my finger badly while slicing ham for Dad's sandwich. It was just after Christmas. The hotplate had stopped working, and Mum had organised for a serviceman to come and repair it.

Dad had told me he was hungry and asked me to make him a sandwich. I was standing at the island bar, opposite the hotplates, focused on getting it right. The serviceman was behind me, working quietly.

All I remember is the serviceman asking to see my finger. He looked at it and said, 'You need stitches. That's very deep.'

And all I could think was that Dad would go mad. I could not let that happen.

I panicked. I started crying. I told the serviceman I had to finish the sandwich. That I would get in trouble if I didn't. What mattered most to me was finishing what my father had asked for. I could not let the serviceman make it. I could not let him take it to Dad.

He didn't argue. He put a cloth over my finger and told me to hold it tightly. Then, without a word, he made the sandwich for me.

When he went to take it to Dad, more fear rose in me. I begged him to give it to me instead. And he did.

He patched my hand with band aids and a small bandage to hold my fingers together. I took the sandwich and gave it to my father.

My parents never noticed the cut. It healed without stitches.

He saw what I couldn't say. He helped. I've thanked him in my heart a hundred times.

Funny thing is, I didn't cry when I cut myself.

That kind of fear doesn't disappear. It waits. It lives quietly in the body.

Just today, I am 66 now, a neighbour rang and said, 'We have a problem and we'd like to talk to you.'

The word problem hit me like lightning. That split second of pure fear. Adrenaline ran through my body. I knew it had nothing to do with me, but the fear was still there, just as strong.

It made no sense in the present. It made perfect sense to the child still inside me. The feeling was the same as being called to the principal's office, even though I never had been. As a child, I had been threatened with the principal, the police, and God so often that the fear became part of me.

The same fear I felt then, I felt again. It still lives in me.

Looking back, I see now that it wasn't just a cut finger. It was the moment I began to understand how fear can live inside you long after the moment has passed. The fear of doing something wrong, of disappointing someone you love, had become so familiar that I didn't even question it. I obeyed it. That day taught me that some wounds don't bleed on the outside. And some acts of kindness, like that of the quiet serviceman, can stitch us together in ways we don't recognise until much later. The fear still lingers, but so does the memory of being seen and helped without judgment. And maybe that's the beginning of healing. Knowing someone once saw your pain and helped carry it, even if just for a moment.

THE COST OF BELONGING

I was twelve, in Year 6, my final year of primary school. Back then, it was customary for the older girls to sweep and clean the classroom. One day, while I was sweeping, two girls who were supposed to help me walked in and asked me a question about another girl in our class. They looked at her, then one of them said, 'It's okay, I won't tell her if you think she's ugly and lazy,' and I said yes.

With that, she turned to the girl and said, 'See, I told you she said that about you.' The girl looked at me and started to cry. I said sorry over and over again. She turned and walked away. The other two girls followed.

I was left alone in that classroom, and I cried. The broom rested against the desk. The dust hadn't settled, and my heart had already cracked.

I wasn't upset about losing a friend; I hadn't had any to begin with.

I agreed with the girl. I wanted her to like me. I wanted to belong.

CHAPTER 3

The girl who was hurt used to say hello sometimes. After that day, she stopped, and I understood why. From that moment on, I made a promise to myself: I would never lie again.

The hurt I caused that girl for no reason was wrong, and I knew it. Even then, I understood what the other girls were doing. They wanted to get out of cleaning, and they did. They left with her and never came back.

Since that day, integrity has been my badge of honour. It was a powerful moment. It might seem insignificant in the grand scheme of things, yet it shaped who I was becoming. One moment. One interaction. One lesson. I was building a pillar of my life, laid down early and learned well. I had no idea at the time that that was what I was doing. I had learned a lesson in integrity, and it came at a high price, paid by an innocent person.

≈ ≈ ≈

For the first three years, I was lucky. My older sister was at the same school. She was a year ahead of me, though people often assumed I was the eldest. Maybe because I watched or carried things quietly. She included me with her friends. I would sit with them at lunchtime. At recess, I walked down to the pitch, up to the quadrangle, past the office and back again, around and around until the bell rang.

The timber floors inside the corridor creaked under my shoes. Each step sounded louder. I was always alone. I didn't look around. I walked, head down. Moving felt better than sitting still. It became my routine, my way of getting through the breaks.

In my second year, there was a girl who caught the bus with us every day. She started pushing me around for no reason, and it was horrible. I remember telling Mum. She said to be quiet and not say anything. Each morning, I went to the bus stop, and the same thing happened. Then one day, my older sister had had *enough*. She snapped and told the girl to stop. The next morning, the girl's mother came down and started yelling at us. Again, my sister stood up for me, and that finally put an end to it.

I was scared, but more than anything, I was grateful. I didn't know how to stop her. She was a bully who simply did it for the power of it. She could, and she did.

When my sister left for business college, I was truly alone again. Sometimes I went to the library. Other times I sat in the chapel, not to pray, but just to sit in the quiet, admiring the stained-glass windows or watching the ceiling fans spin. Occasionally, I would wander into the music corridor and muck about. Once I hid behind the concert bass drum in the corner of the room. One of the older nuns came running down the corridor, calling out, 'Who's in the music room?' I was lucky I was small. She came in, looked around and left. She didn't see me. Needless to say, I didn't do that again.

Halfway through my final year, three girls approached me during a break. They said they'd noticed I was always on my own and asked if I wanted to sit with them. I didn't know what to say at first. I nodded. The relief was quiet and huge. I had been invited to sit and talk, to feel normal, to not be alone.

≈ ≈ ≈

In that last year of school, I was obsessed with my boyfriend. I had met him the year before through my sister's friend, and we'd gone out to Chinatown for dinner. We became friends. He had a new job, starting at five and finishing at two in the afternoon. He'd pick me up from school on his Honda 754 and take me for a ride, getting me home by four o'clock in the afternoon.

He was my secret, and I loved it. We'd often go to La Perouse, sit on the grass, talk, share a can of Coke and watch the ocean. I could smell the leather of his jacket when we sat close. I'd rest my hand near his, and eventually, they'd touch. The wind would blow through my hair, and it felt good to be there, talking, laughing, watching the occasional seagull fly past. It was easy, and I loved it.

Looking back, I realise that much of my childhood was spent trying to earn love, prove my worth, and avoid the pain of being seen as a disappointment. I carried more than a child should, and not only in the physical weight of responsibility – chores and caregiving. It was the invisible burden of unspoken expectations and emotional survival.

What I have come to understand is that resilience doesn't always roar. Sometimes it is quiet. It looks like getting up again, helping again, showing up again, even when no one sees you.

The real lesson I take from those years is this: compassion matters more than perfection.

I may not have always been strong or brave in the moment. I learned that integrity, kindness and quiet perseverance can become your foundation, even when your world feels unstable. Perhaps the most powerful truth of all is that I don't have to carry pain in silence for it to shape me into someone strong. Being seen, being heard and being kind, especially to myself, is where my healing truly begins.

CHAPTER 4

LEGACY

THE SHAPE OF SILENCE

Some stories shape us quietly, while we are still growing inside them. They begin to define the narrative long before we know it is ours.

My father's story was like that. Not only his words, his silence too. Not only what he did, also what he never could.

He was raised in Malta during wartime, a child in a place where safety was not guaranteed and softness had no place. Bombs fell from the sky, and childhood ended before it began. Even if his parents were kind, and in many ways I believe they were, the world around them was not. Fear, scarcity, and silence were his teachers. He never spoke of it. Still, I could feel it in the way he moved, in the way he expected obedience, and in the way he used power to replace vulnerability.

In our house, children were seen and not heard. More accurately, we were tolerated if silent. I learned very young that obedience was safer than

CHAPTER 4

questions, and that compliance was quieter than curiosity. He never raised his hand to speak, only to punish. His love, if it existed, was buried beneath expectations I could never quite meet. And when I failed, even quietly, I felt it. In his voice. In his eyes. In the air.

I have written before about how, from the age of nine, I woke before dawn to wash and dress him, to make his breakfast. I did this every day until I married. It was not requested. It was required. There was no thank you. Only routine. Only silence. And always, the weight of being invisible unless I was needed or in trouble.

I never remember anyone discussing it. One day, the responsibility was simply mine. Mum told me to do it, quietly and without question. I was still just a child. From that point on, I woke before dawn to wash and dress my father, to make his breakfast, to do what needed to be done. It was not a request. It was never presented as a choice.

My siblings were never told to do it. The only change came the day after I left the family home to start my new life. The responsibility was passed to the sister below me, as though nothing had changed, only the name of the one expected to carry it.

Years later, we spoke about it. My eldest sister said it never happened. She said she did not remember any of it. I told her that was because she had been sleeping. My younger sister looked at her and said, 'I saw him wake her every morning. And when she got married, he started waking me.'

That is how it worked in our house. Quiet patterns. No announcements. No discussion. Just unspoken rules passed from one daughter to the next. We lived them, even if not everyone remembers.

I am still amazed that people living under the same roof can hold such different memories. The expectations placed on each of us were never the same. That is something I could never understand. Even now, those patterns have not changed. My mother still believes it is her right to expect her children to do as she says. In her mind, she is the mother, and what she says goes. Age plays no role in it. The expectation is the same. Obedience.

When I had our first child, our son, Dad did not come to the hospital. He did not ask. When I asked Mum, she fobbed me off. By the time I had gone home, I was busy with my son and thought no more of it.

Still, when I had our second child, a girl, a part of me wanted to share it with him. Not out of duty. Out of joy. I had brought a beautiful baby into the world, and I wanted to give him the chance to meet her. He was my dad, and I still loved him. I truly believed he did not know. As we were leaving the hospital, I asked my husband to stop the car so I could show Dad our daughter. I got out, holding this tiny miracle, and knocked on his door.

I walked in. Dad was sitting at the island bar in the kitchen, eating a chop. He did not look up.

I smiled and said, 'We've had a baby girl. I didn't think Mum had told you.'

He said nothing. He didn't ask her name. He didn't look at her. He didn't look at me.

I remember standing there, holding this tiny baby in my arms, not knowing what to do or say. My husband stood beside me, silent. Dad kept eating.

Then, without looking at us, he raised his voice and said, 'Get out. And don't come back.'

I left my father's house in tears. I could not understand. I had wanted only to share something beautiful.

My husband took our daughter from my arms and placed her gently in the car. Then he held me tight and said, 'It's ok. We have each other. Let's go and pick up our son. He's been waiting to play with his sister.'

By the time I had our last child, I never told my father. It did not matter to him. I was not part of his world. He had made that very clear.

Some stories shape us quietly, but their echoes are thunderous.

For so long, I lived within the unspoken rules of my family, mistaking silence for normalcy, obedience for love, and duty for worth.

I see now that my father's silence was not empty. It was heavy with the weight of his own unspoken history. But as a child, I didn't understand that. I only knew that love had to be earned, and even then, it might not come.

CHAPTER 4

The greatest lesson I've carried from this is that the emotional inheritance we receive does not have to become our legacy.

My father's story shaped me, but it does not define me. I have learned to find strength in gentleness, to offer my children what I once longed for: presence, warmth, and the freedom to be heard.

The pain of that day at the kitchen island still stings, not because of what was said, but because of what was not.

Yet even in that moment, I discovered something quietly powerful. I still had the capacity to love, to hope, and to show up with joy, even when it was not returned.

That, I believe, is the true legacy we get to choose. Not the silence we were raised in, but the voice we find in spite of it.

≈ ≈ ≈

I have written before about how, from the age of nine, I woke before dawn to wash and dress him, to make his breakfast. I did this every day until I married. It was not requested. It was required. There was no thank you. Only routine. Only silence. And always, the weight of being invisible unless I was needed or in trouble.

I never remember anyone discussing it. One day, the responsibility was simply mine. Mum told me to do it, quietly and without question. I was still just a child. From that point on, I woke before dawn to wash and dress my father, to make his breakfast, to do what needed to be done. It was not a request. It was never presented as a choice.

My siblings were never told to do it. The only change came the day after I left the family home to start my new life. The responsibility was passed to the sister below me, as though nothing had changed, only the name of the one expected to carry it.

Years later, we spoke about it. My eldest sister said it never happened. She said she did not remember any of it. I told her that was because she had been sleeping. My younger sister looked at her and said, 'I saw him wake her every morning. And when she got married, he started waking me.'

That is how it worked in our house. Quiet patterns. No announcements. No discussion. Just unspoken rules passed from one daughter to the next. We lived them, even if not everyone remembers.

I am still amazed that people living under the same roof can hold such different memories. The expectations placed on each of us were never the same. That is something I could never understand. Even now, those patterns have not changed. My mother still believes it is her right to expect her children to do as she says. In her mind, she is the mother, and what she says goes. Age plays no role in it. The expectation is the same. Obedience.

When I had our first child, our son, Dad did not come to the hospital. He did not ask. When I asked Mum, she fobbed me off. By the time I had gone home, I was busy with my son and thought no more of it.

Still, when I had our second child, a girl, a part of me wanted to share it with him. Not out of duty. Out of joy. I had brought a beautiful baby into the world, and I wanted to give him the chance to meet her. He was my dad, and I still loved him. I truly believed he did not know. As we were leaving the hospital, I asked my husband to stop the car so I could show Dad our daughter. I got out, holding this tiny miracle, and knocked on his door.

I walked in. Dad was sitting at the island bar in the kitchen, eating a chop. He did not look up.

I smiled and said, 'We've had a baby girl. I didn't think Mum had told you.'

He said nothing. He didn't ask her name. He didn't look at her. He didn't look at me.

I remember standing there, holding this tiny baby in my arms, not knowing what to do or say. My husband stood beside me, silent. Dad kept eating.

Then, without looking at us, he raised his voice and said, 'Get out. And don't come back.'

CHAPTER 4

I left my father's house in tears. I could not understand. I had wanted only to share something beautiful.

My husband took our daughter from my arms and placed her gently in the car. Then he held me tight and said, 'It's ok. We have each other. Let's go and pick up our son. He's been waiting to play with his sister.'

By the time I had our last child, I never told my father. It did not matter to him. I was not part of his world. He had made that very clear.

I paid my mother to help look after our son. One morning, driving to work, I saw Dad walking up the street. I pulled over to offer him a lift. He turned, kicked my car, left a dent in the panel with his calliper boot, and told me to go.

Later, my sisters pushed me to visit him. 'He's your father,' they said. I went, reluctantly. He told me I owed him.

That time, I did speak back.

'I DON'T OWE YOU ANYTHING,' I shouted. The words came out like fire, my whole body shaking with rage. 'You brought me into this world. I didn't ask to come here. The only people I owe are my children.'

And I meant it. Every word. Every fibre of me knew it was true.

Later, when he was living alone in a flat, my sisters again asked me to help clean. I agreed. My son was five, and my daughter was one. As we walked up the path, my little boy saw him and waved.

'Hi, mister!'

He didn't know the man he was greeting.

My father's face turned red. His walking stick was already raised. His blood pressure must have been through the roof. When he lost his temper, there was no mistaking it. He was instantly enraged.

'I am your grandfather,' he snapped. 'How dare you call me mister!'

We had not even reached the flat. My sisters were talking to him outside, and I was just arriving. I had not even said hello. The hit would have landed on my son's head.

I never gave it a thought to tell my son this is your Nunnu, or your grandfather. I didn't think I needed to. I was not prepared for what happened next.

I shoved my one-year-old daughter into my sister's arms, pushed my father back, and grabbed my son. I had seen that look on my father's face before. I knew what was coming. If he had struck my son, he would have killed him. And I wasn't going to let him touch my children the way he had hurt me.

After that day, I saw him maybe twice. The last time was two weeks before he died.

He stayed true to his word. He wanted nothing to do with me. He kept that promise.

And I have spent a lifetime trying not to keep his.

THE INHERITANCE

What had happened in my parents' lives that turned love into a transaction and pride into punishment? Why did rules seem to matter more than tenderness? Why wasn't my love, as their daughter, *enough* to soften the discipline they wielded so fiercely?

These were the quiet questions I carried. Not accusations, only longings I could never quite name. For so long, I believed a part of me was missing. Then I looked back. Not at them, but what they had survived.

≈ ≈ ≈

My parents were born in Malta, my father in 1930, my mother in 1938. In reality, the story does not begin with them. It begins with their parents, my grandparents.

My paternal grandmother was born in 1895, my grandfather in 1903, shaped by an era before the modern world had a name for trauma. She was nineteen when the First World War broke out. He was eleven. One stepping into womanhood, the other still a boy. They lived through war, the Spanish Flu and the Great Depression, each wave eroding safety and hope.

By the time the Second World War erupted, they were raising young children in Malta, a British colony that became one of the most heavily bombed places on earth. The bombs fell day and night. Food was rationed to crumbs. The island trembled. It did not fall.

My father was nine when the war began. My mother was a baby. Their childhoods were shaped not through softness, only through survival. Shelters instead of nurseries. Silence instead of laughter. Toys were luxuries. Food was uncertain. Even joy had to make space for grief.

Behind them stood their parents, quietly performing a kind of stewardship we rarely name. Not legacy building, only survival. They grew what they could, repaired what broke, stitched, rationed, endured. They loved through action, not through affection. And they passed on a version of love that was strong, not always kind. Present, not always emotionally available.

My father once said, 'Show your pocket the shade and it will show you the sunlight.' I did not hear those words from him directly. He shared them with my siblings, not with me. I learned them through my brother, and yesterday, in conversation with my sister, I realised he had shared that metaphor with all his children except me.

No matter how I try to rationalise it, the exclusion remains. Whether deliberate or unspoken, it taught me a truth I could not unlearn. That there were stories I was not given access to. Rooms I was not invited into. It was not silence. It was being left out.

Now, with distance and deeper understanding, I see the history beneath the habit.

As a child, I was expected to do many things for my parents. Make coffee. Serve tea. Clear up quietly. Not so different from a waitress. Present in the room, but invisible. And like anyone working silently in the background, I heard things. Not because I was eavesdropping, but because I was there.

I remember one day, I was told I had to go into the city with my father and Nanna. I didn't go to school. I rode the bus with them, walked behind or ahead as they spoke, and later waited on the street outside while they went into a solicitor's office. That night, back home, I was doing what I always did. Clearing up. Mum asked a question. I replied, simply, 'You and Nanna were at the solicitor's today.'

My father flew into a rage. He called me a liar. He hit me. I had no idea what I had said wrong.

Now, as an adult, I understand. Whatever was being arranged that day, it was not mine to name. But I didn't know that. I was a child. I had no understanding of what was significant to him. I was simply answering a question.

There were many moments like that. What seemed small to me was enormous to him. Until now, I hadn't realised that I was always calling him out. Not deliberately. Just by being there. Just by telling the truth.

I was called a liar so often that it followed me into adulthood. I never understood it. When I told the truth, I was punished. When I said what they wanted to hear, even if it wasn't true, they were happier. But I was still in trouble. Sometimes I was left confused. Unsure what was real.

Does that help you understand what it was like for me? Damned if I did, and damned if I didn't. I was in the room. I was doing the work. But I was never meant to be seen.

The apple he pulled from the bin was not food. It was memory. His fury was not about waste. It was about breaking a sacred law: never throw away what might still be useful. I remember that apple, soft, browning, spoiled in places. To me, it was rubbish. To him, it was still good. He would retrieve it from the bin, clean it, and eat the last bite with quiet defiance. Throwing it out meant forgetting, and forgetting, for him, was dangerous.

It was not food. It was his childhood. His mother. The scarcity he had survived. Even a slice of ham had to be eaten with bread, not as a preference, only as policy. Bread stretched the ham. A sandwich fed more than one.

Everyone got a taste, and everyone left the table full. That, to him, was love. That, to him, was leadership.

When I think about it now, I do not feel the sting of what was withheld.

I feel the urge to protect the little boy who never stopped being hungry.

The one who saw one clean bite in a bruised apple as a blessing. I wish he had shared the story. It might have made life easier to understand. Perhaps it would have broken my heart too soon.

Or maybe I was too young to grasp the depth of the hurt he carried. Perhaps silence was the only language he knew.

THE SOLDIERS OF SILENCE

They were never called to the front lines. In many ways, they were the frontliners. They did not wear uniforms or receive medals. Their honours were quieter. The meals they made from nothing. The clothes they mended until they were threadbare. The homes they held together with discipline and silence.

There were no medals made to honour them. None to be worn with pride. They are not celebrated in the traditional sense, yet they exist, and they are visible. Worn with integrity through the very fabric of life, shared in ways no one ever expects.

No anthems were played for the mothers and fathers who rationed food and warmth to their children while their own bellies ached, and their hearts hurt for what they could not give.

No monuments were built for the children who grew up in shelters while the sky roared above them. They were not just denied food, clothing and safety. They were denied the very essence of childhood: laughter without fear, play without consequence, the freedom to wonder, to push boundaries, to be held. What did safety look like to them? They never truly knew it, and yet it shaped them. It became part of them, not as comfort but as a quiet question they carried into adulthood.

These parents, these children, were the true unsung heroes of the perils of war. They carried grief without language. They stitched love into cloth, folded pain into silence, and raised generations on bones and discipline. They gave what they could.

They had nothing else.

They were the soldiers of silence, guardians of what little remained. They did not speak of the bombs or the hunger. They wore the weight of it in their posture, in their rules, in their inability to soften. They carried it without ever truly understanding why.

We honour them not for what they said, only for what they bore. While tenderness may have been withheld, they gave in other ways. A roof overhead. Food on the table. A place where the sun could shine. And the silence of peace in place of the terror they never named. Not for their perfection. Only for their endurance.

They were children when the world collapsed around them, and somehow, they held the line. Their love was silent and giving, unnoticed by the children who received it. That instinct was carried by the following generation, the children of war. For that, they deserve to be remembered.

Silence is not always emptiness. Sometimes it is all someone had left to give.

We are their legacy. Not carved in stone but carried in spirit. In how we raise our children, in what we choose to hold sacred, in the small acts of love passed quietly from one generation to the next. That is how we honour them. Not with medals or monuments, but by living in a way that remembers the cost of their silence, and the strength it took to endure it.

We honour them not only by remembering, but by releasing what was never meant to be carried so far. The rules born from fear. The silence shaped by survival. The punishments passed down without question. Their strength brought us here. Our freedom carries it forward. That too is love. A love grown from strength and endurance, and transformed into a freedom we now enjoy and cherish.

REFLECTION OF THE GROWN CHILD

I used to think I had to become the opposite of my parents to be free of them. That if I loved loudly *enough*, stayed soft *enough*, and broke every rule they clung to, I would be untouched by what they passed down.

Pain does not work that way. It lives in bone, in reflex, in the way my voice tightens when my child cries and I do not know what to say.

I still carry their shadows. The sharpness, the silence, the stories I was never invited into.

Now I see more clearly. I am not only what they gave me. I am also what I refused to pass on.

What I keep are the truths I had to fight to learn.

Love is not earned through obedience.

Presence matters more than perfection.

Silence is not protection; it is a wound that echoes.

What I set down, not erase, only place gently aside, is the belief that I was unworthy. I was unseen, and I let go of the need for apologies that may never come. I stop waiting to be invited into rooms I have long since outgrown.

I still feel the ache sometimes. The hollow of what should have been. Now I speak into that space. I choose softness without shame. I offer my children the safety I once craved. I tell them they are loved. Not when they are good, not when they succeed. Always.

I honour the endurance that came before me, even when it was wrapped in hardness. I choose to grow in the opposite direction. Not from rebellion. Only in reverence for the child I was. The one who needed kindness and became it anyway.

CHAPTER 5

LOVE ON A LEASH

THE PERFECT MAN

I met the perfect man for me when I was fifteen. Everyone had an opinion, the usual talk. They said we'd never last. Seven years between us. Different nationalities. Different families, cultures, expectations. The odds, they said, were slim to none. Fifty-two years later and counting, yes, he's still the perfect man for me.

When it feels right in your heart, you do not recognise it as a thought. You feel it in every fibre of your being. Electricity running through your body. The sound of his voice, the magic in his smile. That is the kind of magic my dreams are made of. I knew then, as I do now. My answer has never changed. When you know, you know. Age has never been a barrier.

Nothing about our lives together was planned. We loved spending time together. It was that simple. Things progressed naturally. We never

CHAPTER 5

sat down to discuss our future. We didn't need to. We knew we wanted to be together.

How did we meet? It was simple, really. A group of friends going out for dinner on a Saturday night, late spring or early summer. We made one last stop to pick up another friend; someone I'd heard much about and wasn't even sure was real. My girlfriend's brother pulled up outside a house in the eastern suburbs. She got out and walked up to knock on the door, and for no particular reason, we all followed.

The door opened, and an older gentleman stood there. He smiled and welcomed us in. And there he was. He was standing in the lounge room, calm, confident, quietly handsome, with eyes that saw more than most people ever do. I couldn't stop staring. His father noticed and asked, 'What are you looking at?' I looked down and said, 'Nothing.'

It wasn't nothing. It was the beginning of everything.

≈ ≈ ≈

I remember the moment I walked into his heart. It was the same moment I walked into his parents' lounge room at fifteen years old. I have never walked out. That day was not about two people meeting. It was two souls recognising each other.

They say that kind of connection is rare. Maybe that is true. Or maybe it only feels rare when few people stop long *enough* to notice it. Maybe it seems rare when it simply isn't loud.

The rest of my life was chaos. Family, expectations, culture, opinions, work. Everything around us was noisy. My soul whispered a quiet truth. A clear knowing.

It whispered, *him*. It whispered, *yes*. It whispered, *stay*. I heard it then. I still know it now.

THE PROPOSAL

It was a Saturday night in November, summer 1975. I had finished work late, around ten thirty, and went down to the auditorium at the Seals Club in Maroubra. Marcia Hines was singing that night. I'd watched her rehearse the day before, and wasn't going to miss the real thing.

The floor was packed. The music was loud. People were dancing. We were standing in the middle of the room, surrounded by noise and movement, when it happened.

She had finished singing 'Fire and rain' from her album *Marcia Shines*. In the quiet that followed, without warning or ceremony, he turned to me, took my hand, and asked me to marry him.

No dinner. No spotlight. No fancy clothes or champagne.

He held me and said, 'Will you marry me?'

And I said, 'Yep.'

Quick. Certain. Steady.

He smiled. 'Do you want to think about it?'

'Nope.'

I kissed him. I held him. I didn't see anyone else in that room. I didn't hear the music. I didn't care who was watching. The world blurred. He was all I saw. That one moment was mine.

He has apologised for it since, more than once. He wished it had been more planned, more formal, more impressive. That I deserved better.

I remember it like it was yesterday. If I had been given the choice, I would ask for the same day, the same proposal.

I wouldn't change a thing.

It wasn't about the setting. It was about the truth in his voice. The calm in his eyes. The weight of the decision already made. That he wanted to spend the rest of his life with me. That was the gift.

To everyone else, it was nothing.

To me, it was everything.

LOVE WITHOUT CONDITIONS

They said it wouldn't last, the years between us, the cultures, the families who thought they knew better. They said we were foolish. Wrong. Too different to endure.

Love has never cared for rules. It does not ask permission. It simply knows.

Fifty-two years later, I still feel it. The same flutter. The same certainty. He is still the one who makes me laugh until I can't breathe. The one whose hand fits mine like it was always meant to. The one who knows, without needing to be told, when the ground beneath me is unsteady.

We built our lives on presence, on the small, quiet acts that whispered, I see you, when words would only get in the way.

≈ ≈ ≈

There was a day, one of those hard ones, when the weight of work pressed too heavily and I couldn't quite lift my head. He must have felt it somehow, that ache I hadn't said aloud.

Late that afternoon, the first surprise arrived. Wild native flowers, enormous *enough* to stretch across three filing cabinets. Not trimmed or tamed, only alive. Untamed beauty, spilling over the edges like laughter I had forgotten how to find.

Two hours later, another delivery. A taxi driver with an envelope. Inside, a gold charm bracelet. Each charm a memory. The Bronze Bomb, his motorbike, our freedom. A Coke bottle, like the ones we shared on warm afternoons by the sea. Symbols of us. Of La Perouse. Of sitting close, talking for hours, the wind in my hair. Simple moments. Fully present. Timeless love. And then, another envelope. The card read:

Dinner. Formal. Just because. 6 pm.

He took me to The Rocks, to Observation Hill, where the city lights stretched like stars beneath us. From the basket he had packed came seafood salad, champagne, laughter that tasted of salt and sweetness. We sat. We talked. We walked. Afterwards, coffee and cake. Simple things. Perfect things.

It was the kind of night dreams are made of. Not for its grandeur, only for its truth. When someone knows how to lift you without needing to be asked. When love does not arrive on schedule or occasion. It simply appears.

Just because.

He has been saying those two words for as long as I've known him. And I've come to understand what they mean.

I love you. I see you. I hear you.

That's the heart of us. The quiet knowing. The steady choosing. The wild, unplanned grace of love that endures.

Fifty-two years on, and it still feels like the first time. The same warmth. The same peace. The same unspoken thank you, whispered between two hearts that never stopped recognising each other.

Love without conditions isn't about forever.

It's about always.

The quiet kind.

The knowing kind.

The kind that stays.

Just because.

THE PREGNANCY AND THE PUSH

I was at home one Sunday, my only day off, talking with my mum in the bedroom when I started to feel faint. A change must have passed across my face. She looked at me hard and asked, 'Are you pregnant?'

I didn't answer. I couldn't. I had only known for a week myself. My husband and I had been talking about it quietly. We hadn't made any decisions. It was a test from the chemist. We were going to see the doctor for a proper blood test. That moment, that question, ended any space we had to figure it out for ourselves.

Mum called a doctor to the house. Later, she told me that my aunty had already noticed changes in me and suspected I was pregnant.

The doctor confirmed it.

I asked Mum not to tell Dad. I begged her. I knew what he would do.

It didn't matter. He came storming into our bedroom, the room I shared with my three sisters, and I was alone. His face was red with fury. I was sitting on the end bed when he entered, and I jumped to the one across the room. He began pushing the beds together, coming at me. I ran. I jumped across the beds again and bolted down the stairs, out the front door, and up the hill.

I ran until I reached the back of the water reservoir, the only place that had ever felt safe to me. A place I had never told anyone about. I sat there, shaking. In that moment, the life we were trying to talk through, to plan for, had been taken from us. My pregnancy was no longer ours. It had taken on a life of its own.

That same week, my parents summoned him and his mother to the house. His father had passed away eight months earlier. He brought his mother and his sister. However, my mother told his sister she wasn't welcome and asked her to leave.

I wasn't invited to the conversation. I was told I wasn't needed. As always, it wasn't about me. It wasn't about us. It became an issue entirely separate from us both.

A shotgun wedding.

The space for choice was gone.

The quiet conversations we had shared were replaced with expectations and commands. Through it all, he stood by me. Quiet. Solid. Certain.

And somehow, even then, I still knew. We would find a way to be ours again.

THE RING AND THE MOTORBIKE

We had already chosen a ring. A simple, beautiful piece we had agreed on together. It was on lay-by. Waiting, like us, for the right time.

One afternoon, my father summoned me into the lounge room. Another tirade. Harsh. Loud. Final. He told me we weren't really engaged. Not officially. I didn't have a ring on my finger. As if the absence of jewellery could erase the presence of love.

I tried to explain. The ring was chosen. It was coming. This wasn't about a ring. It was about him. My fiancé mattered to me. The ring didn't.

My father didn't care. He issued an ultimatum. A ring by the end of the week or there would be consequences. I didn't understand the timing. I knew better than to argue. With tears streaming down my face and my hands shaking, I picked up the phone and passed on the message.

What I didn't know, what I couldn't have imagined, was what that ring would cost him.

Unbeknown to me, he had already gone back to the jeweller. Not to collect the ring we had chosen, only to change it. Weeks earlier, we had seen another ring, the jewel in the crown, sitting in the centre of the shop window. Every woman's dream. He had seen me pause for a moment, smile, and move on. It wasn't the ring we had agreed on. It was the one he knew I truly loved.

I never would have asked for anything that beautiful. It was too elegant. Too much. The kind of thing you see in a window and learn not to wish for. Not from lack of desire, only from already knowing not to hope for what will never happen.

Yet it did.

He saw it. He saw me.

His knowing was quiet and natural. It felt like grace, as if the universe had whispered a truth only he could hear. I hadn't felt it yet, not in that moment. He had. He gave without question.

He sold the Bronze Bomb.

The Honda 754. Custom paint. Matching helmet. Heads turned when he rode it. The first superbike of its kind. His pride. His joy. His freedom.

He didn't sell it out of obligation. I never asked. My father never said the words, but the pressure was there, and it was real. It lived in the looks, in the silence, in everything that wasn't said. My partner felt it. So did I. And still, he sold the bike to give me the best. There was no price. No expectation. It was a pure gift of love. Quiet, unquestioned, and complete.

When I asked about the bike, he told me he had sold it to pay traffic fines. I believed him.

≈ ≈ ≈

Fifteen years later, over coffee with our best man, the truth came out.

The bike hadn't paid fines.

It had paid for my ring.

When he brought the ring to my house, my father asked him what it had cost.

He answered, 'One thousand eight hundred dollars.'

'You're stupid,' my father said. 'She's not worth it.'

There was silence. One of those silences that doesn't break. It settles.

He looked my father in the eye. Calm. Certain. Done.

That was the moment he lost all respect for him.

He didn't argue. He didn't raise his voice. He took my hand and said, 'We're going.'

We left.

Outside, he held me. Not with words, only with arms. With steadiness. He told me I was worth it. That he had shown me long before there was ever a ring.

A hairdryer. A leather belt. Gifts no one else had ever given me. Quiet gestures that said more than words ever could.

We have spoken about that moment many times over the years. Not often. When it surfaces, it still hurts. Even now.

He lives with it. Not with anger, only with a quieter burden. Guilt.

Not for agreeing to buy the ring. Not for selling the bike.

He carries the weight of exposing me, unknowingly, to the full force of my father's contempt.

He was trying to protect me. Instead, he witnessed a truth he has never been able to unsee.

≈ ≈ ≈

We never went back. He never spent time with my father again.
Respect does not recover from a moment like that.
That is the truth that lived between us.
Another truth remains, and it is stronger. He never once made me feel like I wasn't worth it. Not that day. Not ever.
Some loves don't arrive with noise or permission. They come quietly, through steady presence and unshakable knowing.
This chapter reminds me that real love doesn't ask to be proven; it simply shows up, again and again, without fanfare, without condition.
In its silence, I saw myself more clearly. Not only in the story of two hearts, but also in the strength it takes to choose truth, to stay soft in a world that hardens, and to trust that love, the kind that endures, begins by listening to the whisper within.

THE WEDDING THAT PLANNED ITSELF
There was no planning in the traditional sense. My parents summoned my fiancé and his mother to our home, and before I could take a breath, a wedding was being arranged around me. I was seventeen, trying to hold together more than I could carry, and now expected to plan an event I had no say in. It was not discussed. It unfolded like a storm.

It was not about the bride and groom. It was about what everyone else expected.

Amidst everything else, a few moments were mine. We walked to the Greek cake shop in Darlinghurst, just the two of us, and together we chose our wedding cake. I did not like fruit cake, and I said so. The woman behind the counter smiled and gently explained the tradition, how it was made to last, how the top tier was saved for a couple's first anniversary or their first child's christening. She was kind. She did not dismiss me. She explained, and I listened. That mattered.

We chose a three-tiered fruit cake with a little bride and groom figurine standing proudly on top. She told me how to store the top layer, how to wrap it properly so it would keep. And when our son was christened, I brought it back to her. Just as she had promised, she re-iced it. A quiet kindness I never forgot. A promise kept.

That cake is one of the few parts of our wedding that still makes me smile.

I bought the invitations myself, from a pad at the local paper shop. Fill-in-the-blank spaces, written by hand. That was my part. The catering was organised by my husband and our best man. I did not do much. But the parts I did do, I remember.

Ten years later, a friend showed me one of those invitations, still tucked inside her photo album. Her first wedding invitation. It meant something to her. It means even more to me. It sits quietly in my heart, one of the few things that truly felt like mine.

The rest of the wedding did not.

After all the planning and pressure, my parents told us they could not afford the wedding. The expectation was that my fiancé would cover everything: two churches, the reception, the alcohol, the cars, the photographer. And he did. Quietly. Without complaint. Their expectations did not shrink. They grew. The wedding they wanted was grand. But it had nothing to do with us. It had everything to do with appearances.

The reception followed the same pattern. My mother invited over a hundred guests, mostly extended family, without ever asking who would be paying for it. His family was small, and a few came. We invited just seven friends. That part felt real. The rest felt like a production I was placed inside and expected to smile through. It was not about what we wanted. It was about what made sense to them.

No one asked me what I wanted. Not once.

The only thing I chose for myself was my dress. I was working as an apprentice chef, and I paid for the dress, veil, flowers and trousseau with my own wages. That part, I owned.

The rest, that was him.

He never complained. He never pushed back. He never said no. He just made it happen.

After the wedding and our honeymoon, he handed me our bank book. It had both our names on it. The balance was five dollars. He smiled and said, everything I have is yours.

Years later, we were talking about the wedding, laughing at the chaos of it all. Out of curiosity, I asked how much it had cost. He said three thousand dollars. I was stunned. I asked how he managed it.

I saved all my wages for four months, he said. And I borrowed the rest from my mother.

My parents had said they could not afford a wedding. My father had told him I was not worth the value of the ring. And yet, they demanded more than the value of that ring to host a wedding that was never really about us.

And still, we had a first dance.

I stood there in a white dress I had bought myself, under lights I did not choose, with music I do not remember. But I remember him. I remember the way we moved together. Not rehearsed, not perfect, just present. That moment is etched into me, steady and real.

There was a father-daughter dance too. Part of the tradition. Part of the expectation. His moment. Not mine.

There is video footage of the day. My uncle took it. He did a beautiful job. He filmed it for my parents, for me, and he looked after it. He has passed now, and so has the video. But I saw it once, just once. He played it for me, with his young daughter beside him. They had taken the time to capture my story, our story. That was a gift. The gift of being witnessed. The gift of time shared and given.

Those are the real gifts. The ones that become memory. Not always seen. Not always spoken about. But never forgotten.

I always saw. I always did. Heaven knows how much I copped for being present. For noticing too much. For not reacting the way they expected. But the judgement was never for what I actually saw. It was for what others assumed I didn't.

Like all things in life, there are many lenses.

Mine has always been one of presence. Of beauty. Of understanding what others overlooked, and holding close what could never be taken.

That was our wedding.

The one that planned itself around everyone but us, and still, somehow, gave me moments that were truly mine.

THE DIFFERENCE BETWEEN CHOICE AND PROMISES KEPT

The moment the wheels began to move, they moved quietly. There was no grand announcement, no signal. Only motion. Slow at first, then steady. Momentum found its rhythm, and once it did, it carried everything forward.

Perhaps we are not so different.

We like to think that change arrives with clarity. With signs. With certainty. More often, it comes in silence. In unnoticed shifts. A subtle lean into the unfamiliar. A breath held a little longer. A question asked in a quieter voice.

That was how it began for me.

Not with a declaration. Not with confidence. Only with the smallest kind of courage. The kind that rises from somewhere deep when everything else has been worn thin.

I had spent much of my life waiting for a clear moment. A loud yes. A sign that I was ready. Readiness never came. What came instead was stillness. And in that stillness, I felt a shift.

A whisper, rather than a command.

Move.

I didn't know where I was going. I only knew I couldn't stay where I was.

It wasn't about proving anything anymore. I had lived *enough* years trying to meet expectations that weren't mine. I had followed rules that didn't serve me. I had carried the silence of generations and the weight of stories never told. I had learned how to survive.

This was not survival.

This was the beginning of a different life.

Quieter.

More honest.

Mine.

Like wheels turning on a long road, I found myself pulled forward by a force I couldn't quite name. Not fast. Not dramatic. Steady. Sure. Quiet.

That is how new chapters begin.

That is how we begin again.

CHAPTER 6

WHEN SURVIVAL ISN'T LIVING

THE SILENT TERMS OF WELCOME

My life had moved in a new direction. At seventeen, I was married and happy. We were expecting our first baby, and life felt wonderful. What I didn't see, what I couldn't yet understand, was that I had walked into a different kind of control. It looked like kindness. Warm words. Open arms wrapped in welcome. It came with quiet conditions.

My husband's mother offered for us to live with her. We talked about it, and it seemed like a great opportunity to save for a home of our own. We agreed we would cover all the utilities, groceries and household needs. I would stay home, cook, clean, wash and iron. I was more than happy with that arrangement. It was clear, generous and practical. We were grateful.

She welcomed me warmly. Told me this was my home too. Invited me to rearrange things to make it feel like mine. I took her at her word. I have always loved to move things around, to make a space feel fresh. I did exactly what she said I could do. As I cleaned, I shifted ornaments, polished surfaces and vacuumed with care.

Over time, I noticed things I had moved were quietly returned to their original place. I didn't understand at first. I thought I was helping. I thought I was making it feel like home. What I didn't see was that I was unintentionally erasing her presence. I had taken her space and made it mine.

We played a silent game, me moving things, she moving them back, until one day, I stopped. I had an aha moment. Permission had been given. It had also been quietly taken back. It was, after all, her home.

I kept myself busy. I went for long walks. The house was easy to manage with three of us. My husband and mother-in-law left early for work. By ten each morning, the house was clean. I would walk to the shops, pick up ingredients for dinner, and return. Life was simple.

≈ ≈ ≈

At seven months pregnant, I was admitted to hospital with early signs of labour and diagnosed with pre-eclampsia. I spent two months in bed, only allowed to walk to the shower each morning. I missed my walks. I missed the beach. The wind in my hair. The sound of the surf. The days were long and lonely. Other women came and went. I stayed.

Then came the news: I would be induced on 7 October. I was excited. The night before, I went into labour. After a few hours of pain, I rang the buzzer and asked the nurse for a Panadol. She asked a few questions and said, 'You might have the baby tonight.'

I asked, 'Where does the baby come out from?'

She laughed gently and said, 'Love, the way it went in is the way it's coming out.'

I burst into tears. 'No. That can't happen. I don't want this baby. Make it stop.'

CHAPTER 6

She realised I wasn't joking. She left the room, returned with medication to calm me, and sat with me. We talked. She apologised for how it had been said. She thought I was joking. No one had ever told me. My mother and I had never spoken about it. It had never occurred to me to ask.

The next morning, I was taken to the labour ward. My husband was allowed to be there. At 5.45 pm our beautiful baby boy was born. I was exhausted. In that moment, everything else faded. I held him. He was perfect. We were happy.

My mother came that night, along with my siblings. It was joyful. It was two days before my mother-in-law came. Years later, my husband told me she hadn't believed the baby was his. She made excuses until he insisted she come. She visited once. When we came home, she took the baby from my arms to help me out of the car, then handed him back. That was it.

≈ ≈ ≈

Life changed. The honeymoon was over. He cried constantly. They called it colic and said it would pass. Nothing settled him. I asked my mother for help. I was exhausted. She said, 'You made your bed. You lie in it.' I did.

One night, desperate, I put the bassinet in the car and drove. The motion soothed him. I brought him home, placed him gently in the cradle. He woke and cried again. I drove again. And again. Eventually, I collapsed on the bed, fully dressed, and fell asleep.

My mother-in-law found me. 'How could you leave your son crying?' she said.

She remembered the crying. That's what she told people. Not the driving. Not the trying. Not the silence I lived in.

From then on, I never let myself sleep. I tried to do everything right. I kept the house clean. I cooked. I shopped. I folded and ironed. They went to work. I stayed home, did my part.

Every night, as we sat for dinner, she would excuse herself, go into the laundry and make herself sick. Every night for months. A rejection I felt in my bones.

≈ ≈ ≈

For our first wedding anniversary, I asked her to watch him. She agreed on her terms. He had to be bathed, fed and asleep before we left. I had to leave the name and number of the restaurant. I agreed.

We went to our favourite restaurant, Sunar, in Chinatown. We had a beautiful evening. A photo was taken to mark the occasion. We were home within three hours.

As soon as we walked through the door, she was waiting, and she was angry. She told me our son had cried all night and that she would not watch him again. True to her word, she never did.

I was tired. Tired of trying. Tired of being told I was wrong. One night, I snapped. I made chilli for dinner and added extra cayenne to her plate. *If you want to be sick*, I thought, *I'll give you a reason to be.*

That night, my husband finally said, 'Really? Every night you're sick?'

She choked. I stayed quiet.

Months later, I told him what I had done. I was too scared to say it then. After all, she was his mother.

Her tenacity never wavered. I have never really understood her. She held her ground. She let me know I was not welcome in her life. She has never softened.

THE DIFFERENCE OF CHOICE AND PROMISES KEPT

When our son was six months old, I remember turning to my husband and saying, 'I want a place of our own.' I'd had *enough* of living with his mother. It was tense and uncomfortable. She simply was not a kind person.

CHAPTER 6

He looked at me for a long moment and finally said, 'If we are going to move out, I will need your help. You will have to go to work.'

I said yes, without hesitation. I was young, and knew what I wanted. I needed my own place. I needed space. Freedom. That house was suffocating. I could not breathe. I had no control over my life, and no room to make choices that were truly mine. I did not know who I was.

I had gone from my parents' home straight into his mother's house. I had not had a chance to figure myself out, let alone know what I truly wanted. But I knew this was not it. This was not the life I could build in. It was not the place for me, and it was not the place for our son. I was ready to work. Ready to stand on my own two feet.

I spent the next few weeks searching for a job, although nothing came through. His mother, of all people, suggested I try piecework, sewing at home, which would allow me to continue looking after the baby. I did not love the idea. Still, I agreed.

A few days later, a truck pulled up and delivered bundle after bundle of clothing pieces. That was it. The job had arrived. I was expected to complete a certain number of garments every day, while also caring for our baby, keeping the house clean, cooking all the meals, and continuing the sewing after dinner. Weekends brought no relief. There was no off switch, no room to breathe. The days blurred into one long list of tasks, and none of them were mine.

≈ ≈ ≈

One afternoon, while I was sewing in the kitchen, I set the baby bath on the floor with a little water for my son to play in while I worked. He was happy, splashing around with his toys. Everything felt safe. Or at least, I thought it did.

Then the doorbell rang.

I opened the door to find the man from the corner shop, and behind him, a stranger holding my son. I stared, frozen.

'What are you doing with my son?'

The stranger looked me straight in the eye and said, 'Lady, you are very lucky. You see that semitrailer up there?' I nodded. 'If it were not for that bend in the road, your boy would be dead. He came running out in front of my truck. Out of nowhere.'

I could not breathe. I looked down at my son, safe in his arms, then back at the man. I had no idea how he had gotten out. The doors had been locked. Then I remembered the flyscreen. It had a small tear. When I opened the door to these men, I must have unlocked it. That tiny tear had stretched into an opening wide *enough* for him to squeeze through.

After they left, I sat on the couch holding my son and cried. I was shaking. I could not console myself. How could I have let this happen? How could I have neglected our son, so innocent and so beautiful? I felt as though I had failed him. I held him so tightly, I think I may have hurt him.

I simply could not let go.

That moment could have ended so differently. He could have died. The thought buried itself deep inside me, and I could not shake it. That night, my husband and I sat down and agreed that I would find a proper job, and we would place our son into care. We needed help. Real help.

≈ ≈ ≈

A few days later, he came home and told me there was a job going at the deli a few doors down from his work. He asked what I thought. I jumped at the chance. I said yes right away.

I found a babysitter in the local paper. She lived a couple of suburbs over and could start on Monday. I liked her immediately. She was warm and gentle, the kind of person you feel safe leaving your child with. Her son was a few months older than ours. Funny thing, they even had the same name. When you called out, both boys would come running. It was sweet, and it felt like life was finally settling into a rhythm I could manage.

CHAPTER 6

The routine was intense. I would get up early, take the bus to the babysitter's, then another one back near home, walk ten minutes, and catch a third bus to work. At the end of the day, I would meet my husband, and together we would collect our son and finally head home.

At one point, we asked my mother-in-law if she could help, just once or twice, since she was already picking up her grandsons, the twins, from preschool. They were her daughter's boys, born just two weeks before our wedding, and only six months older than our son. The three of them adored playing together. It made perfect sense. But she refused.

Later, when the babysitter had a special occasion and asked if we could collect him early, my husband tried asking his mother again. She agreed, although reluctantly, and that evening she made it clear it would never happen again.

'That boy is your problem,' she said. 'You need to take care of it.'

Then winter came, and with it, an act of kindness I have never forgotten. The babysitter offered to have her husband, who had finished a night shift, pick up our son from our home on his way back. It meant our little boy did not have to be woken early or taken out into the cold morning air.

Such a simple gesture. It meant everything.

That family gave us relief, warmth and the quiet comfort of knowing that someone genuinely cared. Our son was happy. That was what mattered most.

As things often did, it changed.

≈ ≈ ≈

My mother didn't ask. She never did. She stood in the doorway one afternoon, arms folded, voice calm but unyielding. 'Why are you paying that woman to mind your son,' she said, 'when I could be doing it? You can pay me. I need the money.'

It wasn't a conversation. It was a command wrapped in a guilt trip.

That was how she worked. Always had.

And just like always, I did as I was told.

I wanted to say no.

I wanted to tell her that our son was happy where he was. Truly happy. He had a little friend there, someone his age, someone who waited for him, played with him, sat beside him during lunch. They were a pair.

The woman who cared for him didn't just watch him. She helped me. She picked him up when I couldn't. She understood that I was still learning how to juggle it all. She made things easier.

My mother wouldn't hear any of that.

And I couldn't say it anyway. I had never learnt how to say no to her. I was eighteen, still shaped by years of obedience, still afraid of the sting in her silence, the sharpness in her words. Nothing had changed.

So I found myself at the babysitter's kitchen table, crying. Telling her everything.

She listened quietly. And when I was finished, she smiled and said, gently, 'You should take him to your mother. It's the right thing to do.'

She made it easier, even though it must have hurt.

So we took him to Mum's.

From the beginning, it was clear this was not about love or wanting to be with her grandson. It was a transaction. I was expected to provide everything: clothes, nappies, food. The laundry came back unwashed, stuffed into a bag.

She charged more than the babysitter had. And now, without the help of pick-ups, I had to get my driver's licence. We had to buy a second car just to manage the logistics. That meant dipping into savings we hadn't planned to touch.

It made life harder, not easier. And she never took any of that into account.

Worse than the money were the constant criticisms. There was always something: a mismatched sock, a hat that wasn't warm enough, a jacket she wouldn't have chosen. Her judgements came sharp and fast, and I never felt steady under them.

But work gave me something else. Something solid.

CHAPTER 6

I loved the delicatessen. The girls were kind, and we worked in rhythm. I started on the sandwich bar each morning and moved to the deli in the afternoon. I learnt about cheeses and olives and oils and crusty breads I'd never even tasted before.

The customers were familiar, their smiles warm. I felt capable. I felt seen.

At the end of each day, I walked to the butcher's shop to wait for my husband. The woman who owned it had a dry sense of humour and a kind heart. Every afternoon, without fail, she greeted me with:

'Name your poison.'

'Scotch and Coke,' I always said.

One day, she looked at me and said, 'Listen. If you want Scotch, drink Scotch. If you want Coke, drink Coke. But don't insult the Scotch.'

She handed me a glass. Scotch on the rocks. No Coke.

It was awful. I drank it anyway. There were no pot plants nearby to pour it into.

I sipped slowly. Over time, I learnt to tolerate it. Then, strangely, I came to enjoy it. These days, I'm known for ordering Scotch on ice.

She taught me something that day. Something simple, but lasting. If you water everything down, you miss the real flavour.

≈ ≈ ≈

Then, as quickly as it had all started, it ended.

It was a Saturday. The sandwich bar did not open on weekends, although the deli did. I stayed behind to clean, like I always did. The owners' daughter, who was ten, often came in to help. That day, she picked up a greasy, crumpled brown paper bag and asked what to do with it.

It looked like rubbish.

'Throw it out,' I said.

She did.

I finished up, walked to the butcher shop, had my drink, then went home. I was halfway through cooking fish for lunch when the phone rang. It was my boss.

'Do not come in Monday,' he said. 'We will not be needing you.'

No reason. No warning. I was gone.

I stood there, holding the phone, stunned. I had not seen it coming. I had done my job, smiled, said goodbye. I kept replaying the day in my head, trying to find the moment I had messed up. There was nothing. No one had asked me anything. I disappeared.

I cried. Not from sadness. From confusion. I had given my best, and still, it was not *enough*. My husband held me while I came undone. He was calm, steady and kind. He told me it would be all right. Inside, I did not believe it.

I felt completely replaceable.

That same afternoon, we went shopping with his mother. As we passed a small deli with a sign in the window that read *Help Wanted*, she stopped.

'Go ask,' she said.

I did. They hired me on the spot. As manager. I didn't know how to order stock. I didn't know how to run a shop.

I learned. I always learned.

≈ ≈ ≈

I started working at the deli in the summer of 1978. Our son was two years old, and it was my first job after becoming a mother.

About eighteen months later, without warning, I was dismissed. No explanation. No conversation. Just gone. And I never truly knew why.

More than a decade passed.

Then, in the winter of 1992, something unexpected happened.

By then, I had occasionally seen the owner again. He had sold the Mascot shop and opened a new deli at Eastgardens, where I did my shopping every Saturday. I sometimes stopped in for smallgoods. His selection was still the best: imported cheeses, rare cuts, and pantry staples I had come to love. They were part of our home.

I was usually served by one of the staff. I would stand back until they became free. We never really spoke, no more than a hello or goodbye. I always said hello when I saw him or his wife. It was the right thing to do.

One Saturday, as I walked past, he called me over. I went across, expecting just a polite exchange. He was standing behind the counter, serving a customer. Then he smiled and said,

'Tell him the story about how you left the shop at Mascot.'

I blinked, unsure how to respond. I smiled politely and said,

'You're better at telling stories than I am.'

And just like that, he launched into it, laughing as he spoke.

'It was a Saturday afternoon. We had cleaned the shop and Lorraine had left to go home. When I went to collect the takings from the counter, they had vanished. The only people in the shop were Lorraine, my daughter, my business partner, and me. I was sure she had taken it. I went home and told my wife, 'Lorraine's taken the money.'

He laughed again.

'She didn't believe it. She asked me where I'd left it. I told her I'd put the takings in a dirty brown paper bag near the register. That's when our daughter, who was in the kitchen, said, 'You mean the greasy bag?' and I said, 'Yes.' Then she said, 'I asked Lorraine about it, and she told me to throw it out. It looked like rubbish.'

He looked over at me, still laughing.

'We jumped in the car and went straight back to the shop. Dug through the bin. And there it was.

The takings. In a greasy brown paper bag.

Not stolen. Not missing. Just exactly where he had left them, in the rubbish.'

The customer laughed too. And I laughed along politely. It was the right thing to do.

I said goodbye, wished them both well, and walked off to buy a coffee. As I waited in line, the moment replayed in my mind. I could still hear his voice, see his face as he told the story, laughing, casual, certain that I already knew. But I hadn't. That was the first time I had heard the truth.

Looking back, I can say his version of events was accurate. The facts were right. What he didn't realise was that I had never been told. I had learned to hold a poker face from a young age, and in that moment, it served me well. He was none the wiser.

Inside, I felt everything at once: shock, anger, vindication. A bag of mixed emotions I didn't quite know where to put. I had carried the weight of that dismissal for years. The confusion. The silence. The shame that was never mine. And now, here it was, dropped in front of me like a story to laugh at.

And yes, I was glad to know the truth. But I was also angry. Not because he made a mistake, but because he never took responsibility for it. That's what we teach, isn't it? That if you make a mistake, you own it. You apologise. You make it right.

But life doesn't always work that way.

He preserved his pride. In his eyes, he hadn't done anything wrong. Telling the story was, perhaps, his way of making peace with it. But not with me. With himself.

That moment was never just about a job. It was about being blamed. Being discarded. Then being folded into someone else's story as a punchline.

It was not the first time I had been blamed for something I hadn't done. It was not the last.

Now, with the distance of years and the clarity hindsight brings, I understand what that time taught me about life, about people, and about myself.

At eighteen, I carried responsibilities far beyond my years. I learned to survive, to adapt, and to keep going even when I was terrified or unsure. I became resourceful. Not through readiness, but through necessity.

CHAPTER 6

Those years taught me resilience. They showed me how to move forward when everything felt like too much, how to find strength even when I felt lost. I learned to work hard and to take pride in what I did, even when no one noticed.

If I could go back, there are things I would change. I would set boundaries earlier. I would speak up more. I would stop saying yes when my heart was begging me to say no, especially to people who offered help with strings attached. I would trust my instincts over my guilt. I would stop letting fear silence me.

I would leave a few things behind:

The shame that was never mine to carry.

The belief that I was disposable.

The need for validation from people who never truly saw me.

I no longer need to prove my worth to those who refuse to recognise it.

Those years taught me a lasting truth. Not everyone who blames you is right. Not everyone who stays silent is kind. I am capable, even when others doubt me. And strength, once earned, never really leaves you. It becomes part of who you are.

I did not have all the answers back then. I did the best I could with what I had. That girl deserves more credit than she ever gave herself.

I now stand in my own power. A power built not on control but on truth. It is the strength that comes from knowing who I am, what I have survived, and what I will no longer accept.

Standing in your power is not about being loud.

For me, it is about being aligned. It is about honouring my story, owning my voice, and choosing not to shrink for the comfort of others.

The knowledge I have earned and the wisdom I have received live in me now. From that place, I move forward.

CHAPTER 7

FRACTURED STILLNESS

THE STILL YEARS

Buying our first home was a dream come true.

If I'm honest, it was more than that. It was the moment my hunger for freedom finally outweighed the fear. We found it in a beautiful Californian bungalow. Worn and weathered, yet standing with quiet dignity.

From the street, she held herself tall. A wide verandah. High ceilings. Every timber line whispering stories of lives lived before us. Built on solid sandstone foundations, with the only sandstone fence on the street, she had presence.

I used to wonder, if she could speak, what might she teach me?

Inside, she needed everything. The walls were stained, the wiring outdated, the floorboards dull and splintered. She was stripped right back to her bones, almost empty. And still, she felt alive.

She was ours.

CHAPTER 7

≈ ≈ ≈

On -e night, during one of the many cleaning sessions that blurred into each other, we decided it would be easier to hose the walls and scrub them with brooms.

We did, room by room, from the front of the house all the way to the back.

Sugar soap foamed beneath our hands as we worked. Water ran freely through the house and out both the front and back doors. Decades of thick black grime rushed out, as though she'd been waiting for someone, anyone, to come along and set her free. We didn't even think about the electrics. We were young. Reckless. Certain we knew what we were doing.

Painting was worse. No matter how many coats I rolled on, the paint bubbled and peeled. Frustrated, I snapped when my husband asked what I was doing. I shouted words I instantly regretted, hurled the roller across the room and walked out.

Later, we realised what had happened. The original paint, thick and yellow, was lead-based. The fresh paint reacted almost immediately. As soon as it touched the wall, it began to blister. Yellow bubbles swelled and burst like wounds, peeling away in strips. It was as though the house was rejecting our efforts, purging the past in its own way. We stood in the room, staring at the damage, too tired to speak.

Lesson by lesson, we figured it out.

≈ ≈ ≈

My younger sister often came by after work. Our best man would join us. The four of us painted, sanded, ate takeaway on the floor and laughed. No one cared about the mess or how we looked. It was freedom. Four young people and one little boy, building a life from nothing. I was nineteen, and for the first time, no one was telling me how to live.

One incident at his mother's house, nothing worth retelling, was the moment I quietly turned to my husband and said, 'I can't do this any more. I'm going to our place. You don't have to come. She's your mother, I respect that. I can't stay.'

It wasn't meant as an ultimatum, though I see now it may have sounded like one. Years later, I apologised for the way I had phrased it. I only knew I couldn't keep living under the weight of someone else's expectations.

He came with me. And I was glad.

≈ ≈ ≈

The house wasn't ready when we moved in.

There was no kitchen, no proper bed. It had a working bathroom and a roof that didn't leak. That was enough.

I was nineteen. I packed what little we owned into the car, my little V-dub, and set off down the road to my independence. Wedding gifts. Clothes. A cot for our son.

I laid a blanket on the floor for us because we had nowhere else to sleep. For our son, I brought the cot. He was safe. He was warm. That was all that mattered.

Our best man arrived a few days later with a table and four mismatched chairs he'd picked up from a club renovation. They were scratched, noisy across the floor, and perfect. He didn't just drop them off. He stayed. Rolled up his sleeves. Helped rewire the house. Helped paint the walls.

My sister came every night. After working all day at the bank in the city, she'd get on the bus and come straight to us. She didn't stop to rest, didn't hesitate. She walked in and got to work, laughing as she went.

She took on the ceiling – the cornices, to be exact. They were delicate and intricate, a pattern of chequered boxes in an Aztec style. She used a pencil brush to paint every single one, tiny stroke by tiny stroke. It took her

CHAPTER 7

hours. Days. She painted them perfectly. It was a labour of love, and she never once complained.

We spent those early weeks with paint in our hair and dust on our clothes. Music on the radio, late-night sandwiches on the floor, mugs of tea balanced on boxes. We talked, we laughed, we built something together.

It didn't matter that the place was unfinished. It didn't matter that we had no money, no furniture, no plan.

What mattered were the people in the room. My husband. My son. My sister. Our best man. We were all friends. We were building something from nothing – a life, a future.

The house gave us space to begin again.

≈ ≈ ≈

When I turned twenty-one, I decided to celebrate properly.

I had never had a birthday party for me. That day, I cooked, cleaned and invited everyone – family, co-workers, friends. I spent the night moving between guests, serving food, laughing, never quite sitting still. It felt light. Full.

That evening, my husband and I announced that we were pregnant with our second child. It was a beautiful gift. I was so happy, and so proud to be carrying our second child, our daughter, who would be born in November.

Our best man raised his glass and said, 'Now you're really in for it.' And we all laughed. It was the kind of laugh that holds you together, that makes the walls feel warmer than they are.

There was cake, and I blew out the candles. I don't remember what I wished for – maybe nothing, maybe everything – but I know I had most of it already. I had made many wishes, and they had all arrived. They were there with me in the house, as was the start of a new life.

It was a really nice night. The kind you remember in layers: the way the hallway looked in the evening light, the way my sister's hand found mine, the way people lingered long after they'd said goodbye.

I had my family. I had my friends. I had the people who mattered. It was special.

≈ ≈ ≈

My husband gave me a gold key-and-chain necklace and a delicate mesh bracelet with tiny gold beads.

I still have those pieces. They're beautiful. There was a lot of sentiment in that gift, and there still is. He always thinks of me. He always buys me beautiful gifts – gifts from the heart.

The house still wasn't finished, but it felt like home. Safe. Loved. Nothing from my past lived within those walls. If I brought sadness home, he made space for it. Held it without question. Held me without needing an explanation.

A week later, my boss at the deli pulled me aside. Business was slow, he said. There wasn't enough work to keep me on. I knew what he wasn't saying: he didn't want the responsibility of a pregnant employee. I left quietly, holding back tears. A few days later, I walked past the deli and saw someone else already behind the counter. I kept walking.

Somehow, I felt lighter, though. There was time again, for me, for our son. We began taking little adventures together – parks, libraries, walks to nowhere in particular. I heard myself laugh again.

≈ ≈ ≈

As the pregnancy progressed, I began to worry about who would care for our son when I went into labour.

My aunt offered a solution before I even had the chance to ask. She knew I lived more than an hour from the hospital, and her home in Darlinghurst was ten minutes from the Women's Hospital in Paddington. She told me I could stay with her, and she would help however she could. It felt like a blessing. I had no backup plan.

CHAPTER 7

When I told my mother, she dismissed the idea outright. She insisted I stay at the family home instead. By then, she and my father had separated, but they were still living under the same roof. The house had, in practice, been divided for years. Mum and my younger siblings lived upstairs. Dad lived downstairs, alone.

She had a new partner by then and spent most weekends, and sometimes part of the week, at his place. She offered me her bedroom, on the condition that I cook, clean and manage the household while I stayed. I agreed. It avoided an argument.

When we arrived, the fridge was empty and the pantry bare. I did a full grocery shop and cleaned the place from top to bottom. I tried to make it feel like a home again, even if only for a little while.

That evening, she called and told me I had to go. I cried. I couldn't believe that she'd done that, or that she'd said those things. My husband held me, as he always did, and said it would be okay. My rock.

We left. I packed our things, said goodbye to my siblings and walked out. I left all the food I had bought behind. There hadn't been anything in the house when we arrived, and I couldn't bring myself to take it. My siblings still lived there. They needed it.

No matter how my mother treated me, I still cared about her, and about them.

≈ ≈ ≈

I was angry. I was hurt. What she did felt wrong, deeply wrong.

She had invited me into her home on the condition that I help, and I had. I cleaned, I shopped, I made it liveable. Then, with one phone call, she told me to leave, as if none of it meant anything.

The truth is, I could have gone back to my aunt's place. She would have welcomed me without hesitation. I didn't. Going back would have caused a fight. In my mother's eyes, I would have been the problem. That was always the fear. Standing up for myself would only make things worse. I stayed quiet. Again.

The saddest part is that I don't think she saw anything wrong with what she had done.

Maybe she believed she had every right. It was her house, after all. Not mine.

That did not make it hurt any less.

≈ ≈ ≈

I remembered the first time I asked her for help after my son was born. I was young, scared, overwhelmed, and she looked me straight in the eye and said, 'You made your bed. Now lie in it.'

Not to say she didn't love him in her own way. Still, it was transactional. I provided his food. She didn't wash his clothes. And she made sure I knew how much of a burden it all was. It didn't seem to matter that he was lonely.

Years later, when my own children had their sons, our grandsons, and they asked me for help, I thought about all of this. I said yes. Without hesitation.

When my mother found out, she said the same words again: 'They made their bed. Let them lie in it.'

I answered, 'That's your way. Not mine.'

≈ ≈ ≈

As I look back on that time, I see now that I was doing the best I could. I was navigating pregnancy, fear and the need for support, while trying to preserve a fragile relationship with my mother. I accepted her conditional offer. I wanted peace, even at the cost of comfort. I cleaned, provided and showed care, only to be told to leave without warning, as if none of it mattered.

At the time, it felt deeply unjust. It was.

CHAPTER 7

With distance, I also wonder what was happening in her space that I could not see. She was living in a fractured home, juggling new love, old resentments, and a life likely built on her own unspoken disappointments. My independence may have felt like rejection. My reaching out to others for help may have stirred a sense of failure she could not name.

She offered what she could, although it came with strings. Perhaps not from malice. Only from wounds she had never healed.

Still, I carry both the hurt and the clarity that I will not repeat that pattern.

Where she said, 'Let them lie in it,' I have chosen to say, 'I'm here.'

Not in spite of the way she loved, only in hope that love can feel like freedom, not debt.

CHAPTER 8

THE BUSINESS OF ME

THE ORDINARY THAT WAS EVERYTHING

Once we had settled back into our home, my husband and I decided that I would stay home full-time. With two young children, it made sense. I still wanted to contribute, so I became a licensed carer through Youth and Community Services, working from home.

There was a shortage of carers at the time. I ended up with a full house, with up to ten children including our own on some days. It felt like a little community. We would go to the park, paddle at the bay and play in the backyard. The days were full. They were joyful.

I joined a local playgroup through the program and met five other women doing the same thing. We became close and met every day, rotating between houses or gathering at the park, depending on the weather. The children ran wild while we shared tea, stories and the quiet understanding that comes with motherhood.

CHAPTER 8

There were sandwiches, fruit, playdough and paint everywhere. Falls, tantrums, belly laughs, quiet moments and too many cups of lukewarm tea. The children were mostly happy. We were too.

One of those boys, now grown with children and grandchildren of his own, still pops in to say hello from time to time. When I see him, I still picture the little boy I once cared for, now a man. It's a quiet kind of joy.

Life has a way of moving quickly when you're not watching. What felt like ordinary at the time, I now know was everything.

THE ACHE OF MORE

When I found out I was pregnant with our third child, joy surged through me. It wasn't a surprise. We had always talked about having three. Five years had passed since our second, a daughter, and it felt like an entire season of waiting.

The house had taken priority: renovations, repairs, constant jobs that needed doing. The timing never felt quite right. I'm not sure the perfect time to have a child really exists. Eventually, we stopped trying to plan it all. We let it be.

My husband had returned to work after the Christmas and New Year break. The day she arrived, he had joked, 'Don't have the baby today.'

I promised I wouldn't. Technically, I didn't. She came the very next day, two weeks early.

It felt like her: decisive, unconcerned by expectation, arriving in her own time. Like me, she needed things done now, not later. She was worth every minute of the wait. They all were.

Our three children brought a love bigger than I had ever imagined. The kind that doesn't ask for permission, doesn't come with instructions. It fills every inch of your life, whether you are ready or not.

They drove me mad most days. Three little sparks, doing everything they could to keep me on my toes. I spent years in a cycle of cooking, washing, picking up after them, solving arguments, patching grazes, drying tears. The house was full of sound, movement and love.

Even now, I miss the noise, the kisses, the chaos. I miss the way they would sprawl across the lounge at the end of a long day, arms and legs in every direction. I miss them racing through the backyard with the dog barking after them. Tiny memories still light me up.

They had their own ways of figuring things out. I remember them opening the dishwasher door to climb up and reach a glass, sometimes for themselves, sometimes for each other. It used to drive me mad, and it also made me smile. They were helping in the way only children can, honest, unpolished and pure.

≈ ≈ ≈

By the time I fell pregnant again in 1986, life had already changed so much. This would be our third child. Our first had been born in 1976, our second in 1980, four years apart. Now, six years later, this new little life was already growing inside me, long before anyone could prove it but me.

We had planned this baby. Talked about it often. The timing felt right. It felt like the next natural step.

I knew I was pregnant long before it was confirmed. I could feel it in every part of my body. The doctor told me it was too early to tell. I didn't stop asking. In the end, he sent me for a blood test, perhaps just to stop me asking.

And I was right.

It made me feel proud to know my body so well, to trust it, and to be right. That kind of knowing was quiet, but powerful.

But I already knew.

Everything in me was changing, softening, swelling. It wasn't just physical. It was cellular. A knowing that lived in my bones.

When she arrived, our home shifted in a way only she could cause. She was small, four and a half pounds. There was strength in her presence. I never bothered converting it to kilos. The number didn't matter. She was perfect.

Her size meant she fed every three hours. I was breastfeeding, and handled every feed. The nights were long. The days were equally full. There

CHAPTER 8

was peace in those quiet hours, my beautiful daughter and me, teaching each other one breath at a time.

Even then, she was fierce. I would look at her and wonder how someone that small could already hold that much power.

With three children now, I made sure to connect with each of them in small ways every day. I talked to them constantly. I spoke about the weekend, what we would cook, and the smallest things. I wanted them to feel included, not pushed aside.

My husband worked long shifts, sometimes six days in a row. Sunday became our day, the only day we were all together. It became sacred. Not for what we did, only for the simple fact that we did it together.

At night, my other two children would quietly wander into our room. Sometimes they said nothing. They wanted to be near the baby.

When our first daughter was born, our son became a big brother. He would come in while I was feeding her, sit quietly beside me, and watch. There was a gentleness in him.

When our youngest daughter arrived, it was her older sister's turn. She would cradle her baby sister, make up stories from picture books she couldn't yet read, and speak to them as if they were real. I used to watch her with quiet pride. That bond mattered to her.

We gave each of the older children a small gift: a note from their baby sister, cheeky and sweet, saying she couldn't wait to learn from them, especially how to get into trouble. They laughed. In that moment, it felt like they belonged to the story as much as we did.

Even surrounded by all that love, a shift began inside me. It wasn't a rejection of being a mother or a wife. Those roles felt full. It was more difficult to explain. Somewhere along the way, I had stopped seeing myself.

I kept moving. Kept doing. I smiled, showed up, played my part. Still, I could feel the gap – the quiet sense that I was slowly disappearing from my own life.

BACK TO WORK

When our youngest turned two and the older two were in school, I began applying for jobs. I was twenty-eight. I needed a part of life that was mine alone. Not to escape my family. To find myself again.

Eventually, I was offered a clerical role at a transport company. It wasn't glamorous, but it was mine. My first office job. I gave it everything, learned fast, handled problems, found solutions. Bit by bit, I became the person people turned to when things went wrong. I stayed there for three years.

On the Friday I left for annual leave, I felt proud. I was finding my place again.

Then I received a call from the state manager. She had a few questions about the stocktake I had completed. Nothing urgent. Only a quick chat. She asked if I would mind coming in on Monday for an hour.

I agreed. There didn't seem to be any reason for concern.

When I arrived, we spoke for five minutes. I explained the figures clearly. Everything made sense. Without warning, she looked at me and said, 'Your work is not up to company standards. I'm disappointed. I'm terminating your employment, effective immediately.'

That was it. No discussion. No chance to respond. It was done.

I left the building in tears. The job had not only been work. It had become part of how I was finding myself again. I enjoyed going in each day, rising to the challenges, learning to trust my judgement. I was working in freight and had learned how to cost and quote jobs. Customers had given positive feedback. The site manager had commended me on multiple occasions. I believed I was an asset to the team. I had purpose there. I was growing.

When I got home, I was a mess, crying, confused, unravelled. I couldn't make sense of it. There was nothing wrong with the stocktake. Everything I had done was accurate. I kept replaying the conversation in my head, trying to understand what had really happened.

My husband held me. He stayed calm while I fell apart.

CHAPTER 8

'Let it go for now,' he said gently. 'Focus on your surgery. We'll deal with this after.'

≈ ≈ ≈

The surgery had been planned for some time. It was for loose skin removal following significant weight loss. It wasn't about vanity. I wanted to feel good in my body again. Whole.

Late that afternoon, I was admitted to hospital. When they checked my blood pressure, it was dangerously high. The nurse said it was likely nerves, tension caused by the upcoming surgery. I didn't tell them what had happened at work. I was too afraid. I didn't want to risk them cancelling the procedure. I agreed with them. I told them yes, I was nervous. And I was. Terrified, actually.

They were going to cut from my back, all the way around my stomach. The only part that wouldn't be touched was a small section, barely two inches, across my lower back. The rest would be opened, reshaped, sewn back together. It was a major operation, and I was going into it carrying far more than anyone around me could see.

They wouldn't let me lift my own bag or unpack it; they did it for me. They told me to get into bed and stay there. I wasn't to go anywhere.

I couldn't sit still. I paced the room, caught between the sting of the job loss and the fear of the procedure. A nurse handed me a sleeping tablet and told me I needed to rest, or the surgery would not happen. I took it without question.

Two hours later, I stirred and quietly got up. I walked down the hallway, restless. A nurse saw me and asked, 'What are you doing awake?'

'I slept,' I said. 'I couldn't sleep anymore.'

She looked at me with concern. 'That pill should have kept you asleep all night,' she said. 'You were meant to go into surgery and come back still asleep, never aware it had even happened.'

The next morning, the anaesthetist came in. Quiet and calm, he gave the go-ahead.

A part of me let go. It wasn't the medication. It was the silence after everything came undone.

The noise had stopped. The pressure had lifted.

Stillness.

For the first time in years, it felt like grace.

For a moment, I thought I could breathe again.

≈ ≈ ≈

But life kept asking for more. Soon after the surgery, my mother and stepfather asked me to take on a role I had not planned for: caring for my youngest sister and overseeing the full setup of a new restaurant in Bankstown.

She was four years older than our son and needed daily care. Someone to wake her, get her to and from school, prepare her lunches, wash her clothes, and guide her into routines she wasn't used to.

She became one of mine, without question.

At the same time, I was managing thirteen weeks of constant movement. I dealt with tradespeople, coordinated site work, chased quotes, handled council approvals and made sure everything stayed on track. I'd been given general power of attorney, legal responsibility for the project in their absence, and I took it seriously. I did not cut corners. I did not walk away. I was not paid. Not for my time, my effort, or the relentless hours I poured in.

I did it anyway. That is what you do when love is your reason.

One afternoon, pressed for time and running on fumes, I wrote a cheque from their account to cover my land rates. I was honest about it, told them straight away, and made it clear I intended to pay it back.

My mother exploded. She accused me of stealing. Said I had no right.

That moment didn't hurt. It shattered a part of me.

I had kept their business alive. I had cared for their daughter. I had shown up again and again without asking for anything in return. Yet somehow, I was the one called a thief.

It was then I truly began to see it.

When love is taken for granted, it becomes expectation. When you are the one holding everything together, it is easy to be overlooked. I was trying to find myself again. In their eyes, I had become invisible. Or worse, disposable.

By naming the truth, I began to heal.

It didn't erase the pain. It gave it shape: a name, a voice, a place outside of me. I could finally see what had happened not as a reflection of who I was, only of what I had endured.

For so long, I thought being good meant saying yes. Being helpful. Being agreeable. I see now that love without boundaries is not love. It is compliance. And compliance is not the same as care.

I am learning that it is okay to say no, and that I don't need to explain myself when I set a boundary. I can be kind without abandoning myself. Generous without losing clarity. I can give without letting go of who I am.

I'm no longer the girl who says yes without asking what it might cost.

In that quiet shift, a new understanding is taking root. Not defiance. Not bitterness. Only self-respect, a steady love for myself, and trust in my own instinct. The kind of trust that feels real.

I'm beginning to understand that I don't need to earn my worth through sacrifice or silence.

What I need, what I've found, is integrity, self-awareness and authentic presence.

That is who I am learning to be.

WHERE I GAVE MYSELF AWAY

For a few years, life was quiet. We held two contracts, one delivering alcohol, the other beer, and things were humming along. I remember turning to my husband one afternoon and saying, 'This time, the business is about me.'

I meant it. I wanted a business of my own. One I could build for myself. Not for approval. Not to fix the past. Only to reclaim what I had lost. Me.

Catering had always pulled at me. Nights were not an option. My responsibilities at home hadn't disappeared. Then I found a little takeaway shop out west. It was a failing husband and wife business when I bought it. Tired signage. Few customers. I saw potential. A place worth saving. A space I could revive.

I did.

What began as a small cafe out front grew into a thriving business. Regulars at the counter. Corporate catering in the back. A team of seven employees. My husband worked beside me, shoulder to shoulder. We had no days off. What we had was momentum. Together, we built it up.

It made me proud. It wore me out. For the first time, it gave me something I had never truly had before: control over my own life.

The shop was mine. The first thing I had built from the ground up. A tired little takeaway, transformed into a place that mattered. Clients returned. Staff stayed. The space had rhythm, energy. Soul.

What I didn't realise at the time was that it had also become another space where I gave myself away.

It was mine. I had built it from nothing. It mattered.

Still, the essence of me had not changed.

I was still giving more of myself to others than I gave to myself. I poured love into my staff, into my customers, into the heartbeat of the business. But I never gave that same care to the woman behind it all. Me.

The drive inside me, which some might have called ambition, and others survival, was not about passion. It was about proving a point.

To whom? Maybe to my mother. Maybe to the world. Maybe to the little girl in me who was still waiting to hear, 'I'm proud of you.'

Most of all, it was to my father, who had long passed.

I realise now that I was still longing to hear those words from him. 'You've done well. You matter.'

CHAPTER 8

Today, I understand what I couldn't see back then.
I had to be proud of me.
I had to give myself permission.
I had to learn to love who I am, inside and out.
I had to realise that the only validation that truly frees you is the one that comes from within.
Today, I stand tall. I am aligned from within.
Back then, I had no concept of what that looked like or what it felt like. I was building to prove I mattered, when the truth was, I already did.

Even while running the business, I was still quietly carrying the emotional weight of others. My younger sister had taken off across Europe and barely checked in with anyone, except me. I tracked her flights, her plans, her whereabouts. Not out of obligation. I did it instinctively. It was what I had always done.

When our son's twenty-first birthday approached, she told me she was coming home and wanted it to be a surprise. We planned it in secret for weeks. The night of the party, she walked in, home after years away. My mother's face lit up in complete surprise.

For once, what I had held silently turned into joy. No one questioned me. No one blamed me. I didn't have to explain. I stood in the background and watched two people embrace as if nothing had ever been broken.

In that moment, being the one who held it all together didn't feel like a burden.

It felt like love.

MY BODY HAD OTHER PLANS

thought it was a migraine.

At least, I would not have gone to the doctor on my own. I could not. I was very ill. I needed my husband to drive me. He had been watching me push through for weeks. His instincts told him something was not right.

My regular GP was more than an hour and a half away, so we went to a medical centre near home. The doctor I saw was someone I had never met before.

She gave me three shots of pethidine over the course of an hour. Each one spaced apart. But the pain did not shift.

I had suffered migraines before, and pethidine had always brought relief. This time, it did nothing.

I started to wonder if she had actually given me anything at all. Maybe it was just saline. I could not make sense of it. The pain was so intense, and nothing was changing.

After the third injection, I told her it had made absolutely no difference. That was when she said it might not be a migraine after all. That it could be a tension headache. Then she took my blood pressure.

It was dangerously high. This was not stress. It was serious.

She told me I had to go straight to hospital.

I got angry. Told her she was wasting my time. I was in pain, exhausted, and now she was telling me I needed to go to hospital?

I was not thinking clearly. I had been up since four that morning. It was close to six in the evening. I had a daughter at home. My day was long from over.

I was angry, and I was in tears.

I just wanted to go home, and no one was going to stop me.

As we were leaving, she stopped my husband. Pulled him aside quietly and said, 'If your wife does not slow down, she is at risk of a heart attack or a stroke. This is urgent.'

He was frightened. He tried to convince me. Told me to sell. Begged me to prioritise my health.

But I could not hear it.

I was finally doing work that was mine. No family drama. No pressure from outside voices. Just me, holding it all together. I believed I was free.

I was not.

CHAPTER 8

As I stormed out of the doctor's surgery, I remember her trying to stop me.

Looking back now, I see the truth of that moment. I had gone to her for help, but I could not see it. Could not hear it. The help was there, only it was not offered in the way I wanted. I was searching for an instant solution. A quick fix. Something to make the pain disappear so I could get back to work.

I did not have my senses working. Not properly.

Today, I can see I was in a bad place. Overworked. Exhausted. The business was booming and I had been pushing myself too hard for too long. I thought I was managing it. I was not.

When you are blind to what is right in front of you, even care can feel like confrontation.

I was my own worst enemy.

I believed if I stopped, everything would fall apart. What I did not see was that I was falling apart. Quietly. Piece by piece. Behind the confidence and the control was a woman holding herself together with willpower alone.

The body knows. It keeps score.

I did not collapse that day, not physically. But I cracked inside. A quiet fracture I would not acknowledge until much later. A breaking point I walked straight past.

I went home. I did not rest.

The orders were still coming in. The phone did not stop. The ovens needed cleaning. Deliveries had to be made. There were wages to pay, customers to greet, staff who relied on me. And I pushed on, through the pounding in my head, the weight on my chest, the pressure in my blood.

Because that is what I had always done.

≈ ≈ ≈

This was my dream. I had wanted my own business for a long time, and I was successful. I had built something real. Something thriving. I was not going to give it up without a fight.

I had taken the business from a struggling husband-and-wife shop to a fast-paced, fully staffed operation. We had six employees, corporate catering clients, private functions, and a sandwich bar that opened at 5.30am in the morning. The breakfast rush lasted until 10.00, and not long after, the lunch crowd arrived, from 11.00am through to 1.30pm.

Five days a week, I worked that floor. I rarely left before 5.30pm in the evening. And even then, the day was far from over.

There were orders to manage, schedules to confirm, and all the background work that kept the business moving. And when I got home, I still had a family to care for. Dinner to cook. Clothes to wash. Accounts to reconcile. A home to run.

Those things do not disappear just because the workday ends.

This was my life. This was the dream I had worked so hard to claim.

And I did not yet understand that dreams, too, can break you if you forget to include yourself in them.

CHAPTER 9

THE SILENT COLLISION

THE GARAGE, THE JEEP AND THE BOND

Outside work, outside family, there was another part of life that became quietly significant.

My husband brought home a 1944 Willys Jeep, a shell of its former self. His project. Something built for him alone. Slowly, it became more. Not just a vehicle or a hobby. A bridge between father and son.

Evenings and weekends, the two of them worked side by side. They painted it bright red. Loud, bold, unapologetic. Left-hand drive. No power steering. No polish. It rumbled with energy and purpose. Built more with patience than parts, it came to life slowly and steadily. Every piece told a story.

The Jeep wasn't about status or perfection. It was about doing what felt real. It was built for beach trips, bush tracks and camping holidays. Loud, dusty, full of bolts and full of spirit.

We packed it with towels, bags, children and an esky, the dog in the back. We headed to Boat Harbour, or wherever the wind pointed. It never mattered where we were going. What mattered was that we were going.

Everyone noticed it. It wasn't clean or sleek. It simply felt alive. Part of us. Loud engine. Music playing. Children laughing. Dog barking. Wind rushing through the open sides. Towels draped, boogie boards sticking out, someone always shouting over the noise. Chaos. Ours.

We spent many summers down at the beach and weekends away camping up and down the South Coast of New South Wales. Inland too. Gold mining. Fossicking. Sharing slow time with family and friends. Sometimes it was us. Other times the kids brought friends along. There were weekends we got caught in the rain, stuck in the mud, climbing through back trails in the Jeep with nothing more than a map and a guess. Four-wheel driving. River crossings. Cooking over open flames. Life reduced to what we needed and nothing more.

The garage became more than a workspace. It was a place to learn, to share, to grow. My husband would tinker, repair, rebuild. Our son was there too. Curious. Observant. Always reaching. They didn't need words. They spoke through doing.

I would walk out with a plate of food, the girls trailing behind. We would sit nearby. Tools clattered. The air compressor hummed low. I would watch them. Father and son. Shoulder to shoulder. Completely in sync.

Our son loved pulling things apart. Remote controls. Broken radios. Anything mechanical. His father never stopped him. He encouraged it. Supported it. They figured things out together. That's how it worked. They called it a hobby. In truth, it was more. Learning through trust. Growing through presence. Becoming through action.

My role was quiet. Still, I was there. Making the space. Holding it steady.

That's where it started for him. Not in school. Not on a job site. In a small, cluttered garage where he was allowed to touch, test and try. Today, my son builds and restores cars professionally. But it began there. Hands-on work. Silent learning.

There were other memories too. Simpler ones.

They found an old car bonnet and used it like a makeshift sled. After every trip, they would bury it in the dunes. The next time we returned, they would dig it out again. Their father would pull them along the shoreline. Their laughter rose above the waves as the bonnet skimmed across the water's edge. I'd sit back on the sand, watching. Feet buried. Hair wild from the breeze. Heart full.

These weren't grand moments. Not planned. Not photographed. Ordinary days stitched together with sun, salt and togetherness.

Those were the days that stayed. The ones that didn't announce themselves while they were happening. Magic dressed as normal life. Joy tucked into the folds of messy towels. Sandy feet. Family, exactly as it was meant to be.

Even now, they still speak most mornings. Father and son. A quick call. Checking in. These days, the advice flows both ways. They talk about the projects they're each working on. The best strategy for getting things done. It's not corporate speak. Their language is simpler. More direct. Yet, listening to them, there's no mistaking it. The bond is deep. Loving. Equal.

Each time I hear them, I think to myself, we got it right.

Sometimes, the most lasting growth begins in quiet moments we don't even realise are shaping us.

OCEAN WHISPERS

It was Boat Harbour I always came back to.

Not just for its beauty. For the quiet.

The kind of quiet that lives underneath everything else. The mind chatter. The unfinished to-do list. The lingering expectations. All of it softened here.

The rhythm of the waves. The hush of the tide. The soft summer breeze brushing against skin like a whisper.

My Soul Whispered, 'Enough'

Out there, the noise in my head faded. The committee fell silent. No judgement. No performance. No need to explain.

The ocean did not ask anything of me. It simply was. Steady. Alive. Enough.

I've always found peace in its rhythm. A pulse older than language. A sound that hums through the bones. It speaks in a way I understand without needing to explain.

It touches a part of me I cannot name. Maybe my soul. Maybe the version of myself that existed before the noise. Before life became lists and roles and responsibilities.

When I stand at the edge of the ocean, I remember myself.

Not the version shaped by effort or expectation.

The quiet self.

The whole self.

The one who already knows how to be.

CHAPTER 10

LESSONS IN SILENCE

THE TURN TOWARDS HR

It was a friend who gently pointed me in a new direction. She saw something in me I had not yet seen in myself and suggested I meet with a private careers adviser. At the time, it felt like a luxury I could not justify. Still, I went. And sitting in that quiet office, I was asked a question no one had ever asked me before.

'What do you value?'

I remember pausing, unsure how to answer. I had worked in hospitality, managed catering businesses, owned my own shop. I had made decisions, carried responsibility, delivered outcomes. I knew how to lead. I knew how to survive. But I had never stopped long enough to ask myself what mattered to me.

The adviser handed me an A4 sheet covered in words and told me to take it home.

'Circle ten,' she said. 'Then come back and tell me why they matter.'

I sat with that sheet for days. Words like freedom, growth, belonging, loyalty, purpose. I circled some, crossed others out, started again. I was not used to choosing things for myself. I did not even know how to define values back then, let alone explain them. But slowly, something began to shift.

For the first time in my adult life, I gave myself permission to wonder: what do I care about? What do I want to stand for?

It was not about job titles or income or ticking boxes. It was about remembering who I was and allowing myself to want more.

We talked about the jobs I had done: what I loved, what I did not, what had energised me, what had drained me. Then she gave me a list of career paths that matched my strengths and preferences: general practitioner, counsellor, strata manager, human resources.

The idea of counselling felt meaningful. But the years of study and training daunted me. I was forty. By the time I was qualified and experienced, I would be heading towards retirement.

Human resources felt different: practical, people-focused, something I could begin now.

I told my friend.

She smiled. 'We are hiring an HR administrator where I work. It is entry level, but it is a start.'

It was exactly what I needed.

I applied. I got the job.

NAVIGATING FRIENDSHIP AND HIERARCHY

It was a small team, and I reported directly to my manager, who also happened to be a close friend of many years.

That brought its own complications.

Friendships and reporting lines do not always mix. What works over dinner can unravel in an office. In hindsight, it was like oil and water. We tried to keep it separate, but lines blurred. The familiarity that once made things easy suddenly made them harder.

She was managing the team. I was at entry level. The shift in dynamic was uncomfortable. Delegation felt different. Feedback landed differently. I did not want to let her down. I also did not know where friendship ended and hierarchy began.

I had come from running my own business. Now, I was in administration. I was used to making decisions, moving quickly, getting things done. Here, I was expected to follow, to wait, to stay in my lane.

Eventually, a change was made within HR. A new opportunity came up in another team, and I took it. That shift restored our friendship. The tension that had quietly grown between us began to ease. We were able to go back to what we knew best: being there for each other, without the strain of hierarchy between us.

LEARNING THE UNSPOKEN RULES

For me, it was also a time of learning in a very different way. While I had run my own business and led teams for the organisations I had come from, this role required something else entirely. Managing people and stepping into leadership had always come naturally. But now, in an entry-level position, those instincts had to be reined in.

What felt like natural flow, stepping in, solving problems, moving things forward, was often interpreted as overstepping. I had to learn the shape of my delegation and how to work within it. It was not easy. I had to unlearn the habit of leading without invitation and begin again, from a different place.

TAKING INITIATIVE

Then came the day we onboarded ten new apprentices.

I had prepared everything: welcome packs, contracts, documentation, system access, refreshments, morning tea. The room was ready. The lectern was positioned. Every detail had been checked.

The senior HR officer I was supporting was nowhere to be found.

I rang her mobile, her desk phone. Nothing.

People began arriving: the apprentices, their parents, their future managers, representatives from the apprenticeship centre. Someone needed to speak.

So I stood up and did it.

I welcomed them. I explained the process. I guided them through the paperwork and made sure everything was signed. I held the space with calm and care. It seemed to go well.

Later that day, a senior manager pulled me aside. She did not thank me. She did not ask what had happened. In front of parents, staff and external partners, she tore strips off me.

'How dare you. That is not your role. You had no authority to speak.'

I was humiliated. No one asked where the HR officer had been. No one asked why I had stepped in.

When I finally saw her, I asked, 'Where were you?'

She smiled. 'I knew you would handle it. I am the ideas person. You are the one who makes it happen.'

DOING THE WORK ANYWAY

She left not long after. Someone new took her place. The pattern continued. The HR officers delegated work that was not mine. I said little. I got on with it.

One day, an employee came to me in tears. I could not find the officers. My manager was away. So I sat with her. I did not give advice. I simply stayed. She cried for over an hour.

Later, I found out that both HR officers had been nearby. They had come into the room, seen me sitting with the woman, and left. They did not step in. They did not offer help. Instead, they went and fetched a senior manager from another team. She was not my manager. She was not theirs either. But she came.

And once again, she tore strips off me.

'How dare you do that without authority?'

No one asked what had happened. No one asked what the woman needed. No one asked why I stayed.

They simply watched and let someone else deliver the reprimand.

CHAPTER 10

THE ILLUSION OF OPPORTUNITY

At one point, I remember speaking with my manager about my goals. I told her I wanted exposure to the next level, to learn what an HR officer actually did. I said I would like to support a small team, to take on responsibility and grow. At the time, I was so excited. It felt like a step forward.

She responded by giving me a very small group of staff to support. It was framed as an opportunity, a chance to transition, to begin building capability. I was grateful. I spoke about it with pride.

But in practice, it was never real.

The team did not need support. They never asked for it, never used it and were never told they should. It was given in name only. A gesture. A nod. A box ticked.

I remember thinking: this was not about my learning. It was not about helping me grow. It felt like a band-aid. Something done to quiet the conversation, not to build a future.

And I could not help but wonder: was it because they believed I did not have the capability? If that was the case, no one ever said so. Or maybe it was never about capability at all.

I do not know.

What I do remember is how it felt.

How stupid do you think I am?

I smiled. I thanked her. I spoke about the opportunity. But inside, I knew. It was not real.

MISJUDGED BY THE ROLE

Looking back, I realise now that none of my prior experience was ever taken into consideration. All the years of managing teams, running businesses, making decisions and building people up. None of it counted.

I was placed in a low-level role, and from that moment on, I was seen through one lens only. I was tarred with the same brush that so many are: the assumption that your position reflects your potential; that if you sit lower on the hierarchy, you must have nothing to offer.

There were constant reminders. Quiet signals. Small exclusions. The subtle messaging of status. As though my history had been erased the moment I walked in the door.

It felt like an insult.

I was not there to cut anyone's grass. I was not trying to outshine or overstep. I just wanted to grow. To learn. To contribute. But somehow, that willingness was interpreted as a threat.

And I still do not understand why.

Why is it intimidating when someone knows something different?

Why is it threatening when someone wants to help?

Why does the desire to learn unsettle people who have already arrived?

I do not have the answers. What I do know is this: I wanted to learn, and learn I did, in spite of it.

That old saying held true: where there is a will, there is a way.

NO TITLE NO VOICE

During a recruitment process, I once advised one of the senior HR officers not to progress a candidate to a second interview. 'She is not qualified,' I said. 'It will only set her up for disappointment.'

She ignored me.

I was the admin. She was the HR officer. That was all she needed to know. My years of experience in recruitment did not matter. In her eyes, my title erased my voice.

The candidate was brought in. She was rejected. She lodged a complaint.

My manager overheard and stepped in quietly. 'If I recall, you were advised not to proceed. This could have been avoided.'

he officer had more seniority, but she was younger. My experience and my insight were not acknowledged. That was fine. I was not there to be validated. I was there to learn.

Silently, as I had as a child. I watched. I listened. I worked.

CHAPTER 10

REDEFINED BY OTHERS, RECLAIMED BY SELF

Eventually, a new manager was appointed. She called a team meeting. As I got up to attend, she stepped out of her office and said, loud enough for everyone to hear:

'You are admin. You will always be admin. You are not a HR practitioner and have no place in this meeting. You are not welcome.'

I sat down, held back tears and cried in the bathroom.

The irony was hard to ignore. I had taken this entry-level role to build a career in human resources. That was the whole point. I had accepted the title so I could learn, grow and begin again. And here I was, publicly told I was nothing. That I would never belong.

It hurt.

But then I made a decision.

I would find a new job.

And I did.

A human resources manager role. A new beginning.

Leaving with lessons

As I packed my things, the two HR officers who had regularly relied on me came to my desk.

'We owe you an apology.'

'For what?' I asked.

'For doing our job, again and again, and letting you carry it.'

I smiled. 'It gave me the chance to learn. Thank you.'

And I meant it.

Because I did learn.

Not only about HR, but about power. About silence. About resilience. About the kind of strength that does not need permission to exist.

I left that role without all the answers.

But I took every lesson with me, and a deeper understanding of the values I would never compromise again.

CHAPTER 11

THE RECKONING

THROWN IN WITHOUT A NET

I began my first role as a human resources manager with a small printing company. There were one hundred and fifty employees. The company was lean, fast-moving, and full of problems I was ready to solve. I felt prepared. It wasn't just a big step. It was a step I had fought for. However, for all the things I had learned, I still had a lot to learn, and I was about to find out.

He was a bully. Confrontational, loud, used to getting his own way. He towered over me in the meeting room. Saying I was uncomfortable is an understatement. I was terrified. I had worked with all kinds of people before, and I had always been respected as a manager and as a person. But this was different. He came at me with everything he had. The operations manager, who had instructed me to run the disciplinary process, sat silently and watched. He was excellent at running production lines and keeping operations flowing. But he had no capacity, or more accurately, no capability, to manage confrontation.

He found it difficult, and he passed that difficulty to me. Over the years, I've come to see this pattern repeated time and again: managers who believe it is HR's job to manage people problems. He was one of them.

The employee's voice shook the walls. It shook me. I had never been shouted at like that before, not in a professional setting. My hands trembled. I did not back down. That was my first lesson as a human resources manager.

It would not be the last. That workplace had a culture of confrontation. Over time, I would learn that this kind of outburst was not uncommon. I would even have partners of employees come in and scream at me, angry that I would not share personal details. But I knew where the boundaries were. It was the employee I was there to support and manage, not their partner.

TRIAL BY FIRE

Everything came at me quickly after that. Employees shouted in my office. Partners called, screamed, demanded, once for fifteen minutes straight. One partner introduced himself as a manager and told me what I was doing was wrong. He insisted he knew the process. But what he demonstrated was how little people truly understand about procedural fairness and how to manage employee-related situations, something I would come to see time and again.

I stayed calm, explained the process, invited him to attend as his wife's support person, and ended the call with clarity. Then I went for a walk and cried. And the next time it happened, I was stronger. But when the phone call ended, I would walk, shake, cry, then go back in and try again.

I never let go of those moments. I carried them until I grew stronger.

I studied at night. I paid attention to every conversation, every form, every policy on my desk. I read the situations people brought to me like maps, trying to find where to go. I got better.

One of my most important lessons came in a quiet meeting with an employee who had requested a flexible work arrangement. Her husband had been diagnosed with cancer, and she needed time. She began to explain her situation, what she was facing, what she feared.

I listened. And then I said, 'I understand.'

She looked at me. 'Is your husband dying of cancer?'

I said no.

'Then how could you understand?'

I sat back in my chair. I didn't respond. I let her speak. The meeting went on, and I listened. I didn't say much after that. But I heard her.

That night, I went home and thought deeply about what she'd said. She was right. I had spoken to many people in similar situations. I had family members who had faced cancer. But that didn't mean I knew what she was feeling. Each time I had gone through something myself, my own feelings had been different. Who was I to assume I could understand hers?

The next day, she came back. She apologised for what she had said.

I remember my words clearly: 'You don't need to apologise. You were right. While I empathise with you, I have no idea what you are feeling. My job is not to understand it fully, it's to support you, to protect your job, to make sure you know you're not alone.'

She kept apologising. I kept reassuring her. She had taught me something I would never forget: empathy isn't about matching someone's pain. It's about not pretending you can.

From that day on, I carried her words with me. They made me a better practitioner. A better leader. And, quietly, a better human being.

CREATING THE SOLUTION

Training was one of the things I cared about most. I wanted to help people, especially those who had been left behind, the ones without language, skills, or confidence. I approached the general manager with a plan to roll out internal training. He dismissed it immediately.

'There's no money for training.'

I went looking for funding myself. I found it in government training support. It would cover lean systems, efficiency, and job readiness. I built the proposal and introduced Six Sigma, a process improvement method developed by engineer Bill Smith at Motorola in the 1980s, designed to reduce waste and improve quality. It was later made famous by companies like General Electric. I built our plan around it, not just to meet targets but to create real, long-term change.

The general manager approved everything. I asked the accounts team to set up a separate account to manage the invoices transparently. I felt excited. Proud. This was the kind of work I loved, building something that helped people and helped the business.

WHERE IT TURNED

When the invoices began arriving, I submitted the first for payment. It was not processed. I followed up. The accounts assistant told me to speak to the general manager. That was when the shift began.

The general manager, who left for lunch at eleven and returned at four smelling of alcohol, told me he no longer trusted what I was doing. He said he wanted to performance manage me. He wanted full visibility. He wanted to know where the money had gone.

I brought him the paperwork, the approval letters, the government funding agreement, the payment request. I reminded him that I had asked for a dedicated account to manage training payments. It had never been set up.

He waved me off. 'I'll take care of it.'

The next invoice came, still unpaid. I followed up again. The finance manager said it was not her responsibility.

THE CHOICE

I returned to the general manager. This time, he looked me in the eye.

'It's none of your business what I've done with the money. When the government asks, I'll say I don't know. I'll say you spent it.'

I stood there, trying to process what I had heard. Then I walked out of his office and resigned. No negotiations. No backup job. I simply left.

That was a line I would not cross.

When I arrived home, I called the government department that had provided the funding. I told them what had happened and submitted all the documentation. Months later, an investigator contacted me. I gave my full statement. Nothing came of it.

I did not regret it. I may have walked away without a job. I walked away with my integrity.

For the first time in a long while, I had not merely survived. I had stood my ground.

It was never just about one man's behaviour. It was about a system that tolerated silence, avoided conflict, and shifted accountability onto the wrong shoulders. I left that office knowing I had done the right thing, not because it was easy, but because I was willing to lose the job to keep what mattered more.

Integrity was the line I would never cross.

CHAPTER 12

THE RETURN

A JUST EXIT

After I left the printing company, I quickly secured another position, this time as a human resources manager for a national maintenance business. I was responsible for more than a thousand employees, supporting operations across the eastern seaboard, from Darwin to Albury–Wodonga.

It was a solid role. My manager was strong and fair. The work was broad, meaningful and complex. I travelled across the country for site visits and attended monthly meetings in Melbourne. Finally, I was using my experience in ways that mattered. I felt capable. I felt valued.

Then the company restructured. My position remained the same in title, although the substance was quietly stripped away. Without discussion or warning, my responsibilities were handed to a younger, less experienced graduate. I was no longer needed.

While I had a strong case for reinstatement, I did not want to risk tarnishing my reputation within the HR industry. It is a small community.

I rang a friend, the same one who had helped me enter human resources years earlier. I explained what had happened. She said, 'Start contracting. There is always work. You will learn so much.'

She was right. The next three years were filled with contract work.

THE GIFT OF HARD LESSONS

I had worked as a manager with my own human resources team. Safety, workers' compensation, industrial and employee relations were all my responsibility. I worked in many government roles: local, state and federal. They were always looking for contractors. It was easy. I had learned early in my career how to figure things out, how to make things work.

When my friend said, 'Do contract work, you'll learn,' I listened. And I did learn. They handed me, the contractor, everything they could not manage themselves. I took it on, never saying no. Those problems were gifts tied up with big bows.

Time and time again, they asked me to stay. They gave me more. No one asked for proof. They pointed to a desk and said, 'That's yours.' I sat down and got to work.

Eventually, I reached a point where I wanted to settle down again. I applied for a permanent position: Head of Human Resources, Industrial and Employee Relations. It was a mid-level management role, and I got the job. I had a small team, and we worked well together.

They advertised the Human Resources Manager position. I did not apply. I was happy where I was. When the new manager was appointed, she called me into her office. We spoke about my career aspirations. I was clear, and I was glad she seemed interested in building the team. I told her I wanted to support her move into the director role and be part of the succession plan for her position across the department. She nodded, smiled, and said we could work together.

CHAPTER 12

For a few months, everything went well. Then, one morning, she walked in and announced that she was calling an 8 am meeting every day. We were to provide a list of our work for the day.

I went to the first meeting and advised that I had pre-arranged early industrial meetings with the union and would be up to ten minutes late. These meetings were off-site and could not be moved. She lost her temper and told me to cancel all my meetings, regardless of when they were arranged. She said I could not be late.

I called and left her a message, explaining that I could not reach the union organiser for the following morning and that the employee involved wanted a delegate. I said I would do my best to be on time. She did not respond.

I arrived fifteen minutes late. She reprimanded me in front of the team. From then on, I was required to report to her daily at 4.30 pm to explain what I had completed and what remained outstanding.

I complied. Nothing was ever good enough. I explained that much of my role involved impromptu meetings with senior managers. She did not care. She told me I was incompetent. She began giving all my industrial relations work to a new contractor. She ignored me in meetings and accused me of being untrustworthy. She required me to submit all correspondence to her before sending it out.

One afternoon, around 1 pm, I asked her for a finalised letter that had been with her for a week. I was scheduled to attend a final meeting with the operations manager to close an industrial matter. She snapped.

'You are not my manager. How dare you ask for the letter.'

She told me she did not have time to read it. Then she screamed at me in the middle of the office. She told me to cancel the meeting.

I felt small. Like a child. I could not go to the meeting. I didn't have the letter. I wasn't allowed.

I got up and walked out. I did not go back.

INTEGRITY AS A COMPASS

I did, however, ask for an independent investigation. When the findings came back, the general manager asked to meet with me. She said there was no evidence that bullying had occurred. She wanted me to return to work when I was feeling better.

I looked at her and, without thinking, said, 'Are you fucking kidding me?'

She said she could not dismiss the employee. I told her I had never asked for that. I could not, and would not, work with that person. She would have my resignation that day. She asked me to reconsider. I said no.

The following Monday, one of the women who had worked under me called. They had terminated the Head of Human Resources. I thanked her for calling and said nothing more.

The person who had hired me later rang and asked me to return, even as a contractor. I refused. It was still too raw. Months later, she called again. This time she was frank. One of the cases I had been managing had reached the Anti-Discrimination Board, the Industrial Commission and SafeWork. The previous HR manager and the contractor had mismanaged my investigation. I was the only one who could answer the questions.

I agreed to return.

The man involved had not been a pleasant person. He had made false allegations. I believed in doing the right thing.

I went back. Faced all the tribunals. Answered the questions. Fixed the problem.

The employee abused me throughout the process, blaming me. That, I could live with. He did not understand the mess behind the scenes.

He had a right to be angry, although not to treat me that way. That seemed to be my lot. I did not go back for him. I went back in the hope of sparing others from suffering. I have never wanted people to be left in pain when I could help. I took on the work I did to support others and to leave places better than I found them.

CHAPTER 12

That man was not kind. What he had been accused of was a fabrication. The others did not like him. The accusation they made could have cost him his livelihood. That was wrong. Integrity is why I went back. Integrity is a line I do not cross. I learned that lesson in primary school, and have never forgotten it.

In the end, I moved on. It was time. I needed to step away from the past. I still carried feelings I had not resolved, threads I did not know how to repair. I had learned how to move house, how to start again. I had not yet learned how to mend what was broken inside me. That is why I left for good this time.

I thought that by leaving, I had protected myself. But I was only repeating the pattern. Survive. Rebuild. Stay silent. It looked like strength. Inside, I was still carrying pieces I didn't know how to set down.

From a young age, I had learned how to shrink. How to comply. How to keep the peace. Now, I was learning how to stand. And standing, even alone, is its own kind of legacy.

≈ ≈ ≈

Integrity rarely announces itself.

It lives in small, private choices. The ones no one witnesses, yet they shape who we become.

Standing tall does not always look like strength. Sometimes, it looks like walking away quietly, knowing you did not bend.

The cost is real. But so is the peace that follows.

In time, the noise fades.

What remains is the quiet truth that you stayed aligned, even when no one was watching.

CHAPTER 13

THE MOUNTAIN AND THE LANDSLIDE

THE MEASURE OF A LEADER

The next role I stepped into supported a large national programme aligned with a federal agency. High stakes. High pressure. High volume. Many would have stepped back. I stepped forward.

A new general manager had joined the organisation a week before me. We clashed early on. Over time, we found our rhythm. We didn't always agree. We debated almost everything, and always with merit. We challenged each other. Because of that, we reached good outcomes, fair outcomes. He fought for his employees. He engaged, enabled and empowered people.

He taught me a different kind of management. One that believed in people and gave second chances where others would not. The rewards of that approach returned a hundredfold. If he asked someone to move a mountain, they would, because they trusted him.

CHAPTER 13

I worked under him for three years. My hours were long-starting between four and seven in the morning and finishing by half past five. I was deeply invested. I managed complex employee issues, industrial relations cases and rebuilt broken systems at site level. I didn't only train people; I coached them. I taught managers how to manage, how to think, how to listen. I changed the way we delivered Management 101.

When I sat in on my first Management 101 session, I saw what was missing. It was scripted, recycled, and uninspired. One supervisor said, 'We can read the slides as well as they can read them to us.' That was all I needed.

I redesigned the entire programme-coaching over content, conversation over compliance. We built real dialogue. Real learning. People didn't just attend-they engaged. They sent feedback. They started speaking up. And they started owning the culture they were part of.

What began as mandatory training became something else entirely. It became movement.

The shift was real. And, like many shifts, it came at a cost.

It was May 2022 when I received a call from my direct manager. She said she wanted to have a chat. I told her I was heading out to collect the keys to our new home. She said, 'No worries, I'll call you later this afternoon.' We agreed.

At 6.30 p.m. that evening, she called me back.

She told me she wanted to have an off-the-record conversation. That while I was one of the hardest-working employees she had ever worked with, I was not what they required in the business. She asked me to resign my job. If I refused, she said, she would make it very uncomfortable for me. Not termination-just pressure. Enough to make staying untenable.

She said the site manager had argued with her when she called to tell him. He had pushed back. He wasn't happy. He had gone to the general manager and fought for me. She said he had done all he could.

She told me the general manager was fully aware, and that I could call him. So I did.

He said he was sorry. He confirmed what I had been told. He had taken it to the Director of Human Resources. He had done everything he could.

He was more than a colleague. Over time, he had become a friend. It was the first time in my career that someone saw the true value I was adding-and went to bat for me.

I resigned.

I worked my final week from home. I didn't speak to anyone. On my last day, I packed my office quietly and left.

'This isn't goodbye,' he said. 'We'll talk.'

And he meant it. He stood behind me. He went to bat for me. He was the kind of man people would leave jobs to follow.

I drove away hollow.

A chapter had been taken from me. But the work I built-those conversations, those systems, those people-still stands. Even if I'm no longer part of it.

What I taught wasn't just workplace process. It was life: how to lead, how to listen, how to stand up.

While the work was hard and relentless, I loved it. I loved the people. The place had a heart. Yes, we struggled. Yes, we challenged each other. But we became something more than colleagues-we became a kind of family. It was one of the best places I had ever worked. The staff and management team at the centre made me feel welcome, respected and appreciated.

They didn't just connect with their staff-they changed how performance was managed. Leadership shifted. Not just good leadership-great leadership. They learned how to hold critical conversations that created change, not just enforce discipline. Conversations that shaped culture. Conversations that built trust.

That, perhaps, is the truest kind of legacy.

UNSEEN, UNHEARD, UNDONE

The role came through a quiet referral, a nod from an industrial lawyer who had seen my work and believed I could help untangle the workplace. I was

CHAPTER 13

placed into the position temporarily at first. Later, I formally applied for the permanent role and was awarded the position on merit.

When I stepped in, I did so as I always had, with a genuine belief that I could make a difference. That the work mattered. That people mattered.

It didn't take long to realise the workplace was riddled with deep unrest. A culture that fed on silence, fear and quiet compliance. The union held a generational grip on decisions, dynamics and dialogue. What I uncovered wasn't just broken systems; it was a culture of fear that silenced people before they could speak.

The first vote of no confidence came within just a few months. I had seen the union play these games before, but this was different. This was targeted. I hadn't complied early on, and they knew I could see the strategy.

When you challenge power, you step into the firing line. That is the cost of breaking silence.

Still, we weren't alone. We were a team then. People began to trust us. They shared stories that had lived underground for years, believing, for the first time, that someone might listen.

The acting CEO saw the damage. He didn't dismiss it. When the vote of no confidence was lodged, it went to the Commission. The Commissioner found it held no legal standing and ordered it withdrawn. The retraction was public, but not in good faith.

I took it on the chin. At the time, it felt like part of the job.

The Commission also recommended off-the-record mediation. I wasn't obligated to attend, but I agreed. It felt like a chance to do what I came for: untangle the mess at its root.

Over the course of the afternoon, I sat with the Commissioner and listened. We unpacked stories. It became clear that the vote wasn't about me. It was history repeating, fractures that predated my arrival.

Still, the process drained me. And it marked the start of something deeper. Not just industrial unrest. Cultural unravelling.

Then the CEO changed. And with him, everything else.

He arrived without introduction. I was called into a meeting. No welcome. No context. Just instruction.

'I know who you are,' he said.

The message was clear. There was no curiosity. Just certainty.

I was instructed to vacate my office and relocate to head office, away from the people I was hired to support. I was no longer permitted to speak to them. Not even in greeting.

Emails stopped. Meeting invites disappeared. I was excluded from briefings I used to lead.

I had been erased. Quietly. Efficiently. As if I had never been there at all.

The HR team began to fracture. New people arrived. I was told, indirectly, that they would now perform my role. I was expected to help onboard them. To guide them. To serve.

The acting supervisor relished her new authority. I didn't respect her, not because of her title, but because of how she used it. She was being used, and I could see it. She couldn't.

I was no longer allowed in my old office. It became a shared meeting space. My belongings were to be removed.

I never removed them. I remember standing outside the glass wall of that office, the space where I used to work, once visible, part of the team. I stood there and listened to laughter rise from the other side. Laughter that once included me.

But that was the past.

Now, I sat in a storeroom at head office. Brick walls. Timber door. A space never meant to be an office. A space where I was no longer seen at all. Silence wrapped around me like insulation.

One small window. Life moving on outside. Buses. People. Reminders that I still existed.

Sometimes I stepped outside just to see faces. Not to speak. Just to be near someone. Anyone. I'd call my husband. Cry. Breathe. Wash my face in

CHAPTER 13

the shopping centre bathroom. Then return to the room and hold together what hadn't yet fallen apart.

Still, I kept trying to do the work.

I was expected to lead a major industrial investigation. I was the subject matter expert. But I had only been there nine months. I had already been segregated from the work I was hired to do. And now, I was tasked with carrying a case I never should have held.

That afternoon, I was asked to lead a grievance investigation. But I wasn't permitted to speak to the manager involved, nor to the employee who had lodged the grievance. When I asked the acting supervisor for clarity, she said, 'Technically you can talk to them, but you're not supposed to.'

Earlier that same day, I had been contacted by the PA to discuss an upcoming breakfast briefing. She confirmed I had received the invitation and then informed me I was not welcome. I was ordered not to attend.

And then, hours later, I was told the union, the same union that had orchestrated multiple votes of no confidence in me, that had watched me disappear without a word, now wished to 'work collaboratively' with me.

To add insult to injury, I was also informed that a key employee, someone I had spent six months supporting through return to work, had vanished again. I was asked to fix it. But I wasn't allowed to speak to them either.

I was being handed complex, sensitive matters to resolve and simultaneously stripped of the very access required to do my job.

It was absurd. It was cruel. And it was intentional.

That day, I couldn't bring myself to go into the office. I stayed home and worked from my desk. The calls came through one by one: the breakfast briefing I was disinvited from, the investigation I was expected to manage without access to the people involved, and finally, the union's sudden desire to work collaboratively with me.

I was unravelling, but quietly. Until I wasn't.

I don't remember the moment I broke, only the sound: my own voice, crying uncontrollably. My husband found me in the room.

'We're going to the doctor,' he said.

I don't remember leaving the house. I don't remember the drive. I don't remember what I said to the doctor. Only this: my hands over my face, my body trembling, and the words spilling out of me again and again, *I can't do this anymore.*

That's what I remember.

Not what was asked. Not what was prescribed. Just the knowing, deep in my body, that I was done.

Done pretending I could hold it together. Done carrying what had never been mine to carry alone.

The months that followed were not restful. They were fractured. *I had been holding on so tightly for so long that when I let go, I collapsed inward.*

One day, as my husband and I were driving, I saw a vehicle from the organisation on the road. My breath caught. My chest tightened. My vision blurred. I wasn't driving. I hadn't been since the collapse. I had lost my confidence completely.

My husband had become my driver. He took me to every appointment, every outing. That moment in the car, I broke again.

An anxiety attack.

It was not the first, and it would not be the last.

It wasn't just the anxiety. I ranted. I raved. I didn't want to be seen. Not by anyone.

Today, I understand that response. But at the time, all I knew was that I couldn't bear to exist in their world anymore. I didn't want to be talked about. I didn't want sympathy. I didn't want to be found.

The hurt ran that deep.

I wanted to disappear. And for a while, I did.

Another time, I was invited to a breakfast briefing, I thought I was ready. But halfway through, the room spun. I left. I wandered the city in tears. *Couldn't speak. Couldn't breathe. Couldn't find my way back.*

That was another.

CHAPTER 13

I avoided going out. Familiarity sent me spiralling. I had given everything and been discarded like a problem no one wanted to own.

At home, I tried to find a way back. I sat at my desk and started typing policies. I don't know why. There was no audience, no purpose. Just the act of writing something structured. Anything to feel my way back to language. To identity.

With time, therapy and support, the fog began to lift. A psychologist. A psychiatrist. A mentor who reminded me who I had been.

They didn't fix me. *They helped me remember.*

I learned to journal. To meditate. To sit in stillness without being swallowed.

I found who I was beneath the noise, the pressure, the armour. It wasn't easy. It wasn't quick.

But *I came home to myself.*

Not through fanfare or defiance.

Through stillness. Through breath.

Through choosing not to chase worth I had already earned.

And in that quiet, *I discovered a strength I didn't know I had.*

The strength to simply be.

And to know that *it was enough.*

CHAPTER 14

THE QUIET RETURN

NOT STARTING OVER; STARTING DIFFERENTLY

I used to think every departure meant beginning again. A new job. New people. New rules. I used to pack away parts of myself with every move. I no longer do that.

This time, I didn't start over. I started differently. I didn't rush to prove anything. I didn't make myself smaller to fit into someone else's shape. I walked in with a quiet knowledge. I knew who I was, and I was done asking for permission to be that person.

The job wasn't perfect. None ever are. But it was mine. On my terms. I set clear boundaries, and when people tested them, I didn't flinch. I'd learned to listen without absorbing. To respond without explaining. To be kind without overextending.

WORK AS A MIRROR

Work has always been more than work to me. It has been a mirror, sometimes clear, sometimes warped, reflecting what I believed about myself.

For a long time, I believed I had to earn my place every day. That I needed to be grateful, agreeable, tireless. That belief is gone now. I've replaced it with a truth quieter, yet stronger.

I belong where I stand. Not by permission. By choice.

People noticed the difference. Some were drawn to it. Others were challenged by it. That was no longer my responsibility to manage.

I wasn't chasing roles anymore. I was choosing alignment

THE POWER OF NOT EXPLAINING

There is a strange power in not explaining yourself. In letting silence do the work.

When someone questioned a decision, I listened. I considered. And when I was clear, I didn't justify. I moved forward.

It unsettled people. Especially those used to me softening my tone, cushioning the truth, over-communicating to keep the peace. I had spent too many years giving away my clarity to keep others comfortable.

Now I keep it close.

THE KIND OF LEADER I BECAME

Being human is messy. I've learned to be okay with that, and that's a good thing. I'd rather be real than polished. If I were polished, people wouldn't come and speak to me.

Leadership is often spoken of in loud terms: direction, command, authority. But that has never been the kind of leader I wanted to be.

I wanted to be the kind who sees people. The kind who asks real questions. Who listens to understand, not just to respond. I wanted to leave rooms better than I found them, even if no one noticed.

I began to lead with stillness, with clarity, with conviction that did not need to announce itself.

People began to trust that if I said I would do something, I did. If I said no, it meant no. There was a quiet relief in that kind of consistency, both for them and for me.

WHAT I NO LONGER CARRY

I no longer carry the weight of other people's discomfort. I no longer carry the need to prove I am good, competent or kind. I know these things to be true, and that is enough.

I no longer say yes to be liked. I no longer say sorry for having boundaries.

I no longer wait for permission to rest. To speak. To lead. To leave.

I have set all of that down, gently, piece by piece.

RECLAIMING THE SELF

Healing did not come all at once.

It came in pauses. In walks outside at lunchtime. In saying no without guilt. In not reacting. In noticing how my breath changed when someone raised their voice. In choosing not to match their energy.

It came in the quiet realisation that I did not have to keep surviving. I could begin living.

Not everyone understood the change. Some missed the version of me that was easier to manage. I did not miss her.

I was not rebuilding anymore. I was reclaiming.

THE STRENGTH IN QUIET RESOLVE

Sometimes, strength is not loud. It is not in the fight or the walkout or the bold speech.

Sometimes, strength is what you no longer carry.

It is what you no longer explain. What you no longer tolerate. What you no longer chase.

CHAPTER 14

There is power in being gentle with yourself, even when the world has been sharp.

There is power in standing still, especially when you have spent years running.

And there is power in knowing you are whole. Not through validation from someone else. Through the choice to believe it yourself.

PROLOGUE

THE BEGINNING OF ALIGNMENT

It wasn't a crash. Not a collapse. Just a light, quietly turning on.

There was no single moment that told me things had changed. Just a gentle unfolding. A stillness that felt different. I was sitting at my desk, surrounded by the hum of a day like any other, when something shifted. It wasn't dramatic. It was subtle. But it was there. A quiet sense that something in me had realigned. Not by force. By truth.

I found myself reflecting on the work I've been doing through Balance Point Solutions®. Work I once approached with urgency, driven by proof and performance. Now it felt different. Calmer. More grounded. Less about holding everything together and more about standing fully in what I knew.

What I was building wasn't just a business. It was a reflection of what I had lived through and how I had found my way home.

Still, the question surfaced.

Is this just another place where I give myself away?

It was a fair question. I had given myself away in many places before. In roles, relationships, responsibilities and silence. I had handed over my energy, my clarity and my sense of self, quietly and completely. All in the name of being useful. Being enough.

The answer came gently, and this time I trusted it.

No. This is not the same.

PROLOGUE

There was a time I believed that struggle was the price of meaning. That in order to serve well, I had to suffer quietly. I believed that to matter, I had to hold everything and everyone together, even when I was coming undone.

You know the signs. You may have lived them too. The long hours. The collapsing boundaries. The tightness in the chest. The migraines. The breath you keep forgetting to take. The voice that says, *'Just keep going'*, even when there is nothing left to push from.

My breaking wasn't loud. It didn't come with noise or drama. It came in the quiet. In the mirror. In the slow and certain knowing that I no longer recognised myself. Not in the way I moved. Not in the way I led. Not in the way I lived.

That was the fall.

The rise was slower. Quieter. Uneven and deeply human.

It came in moments. I rested when I wanted to run.

I said no when it would have been easier to say yes.

I let go of roles that once defined me but no longer served me.

I stopped performing strength. I stopped performing leadership.

I stopped performing myself.

In that stillness, I began to rebuild.

Balance Point Solutions® wasn't born from strategy.

It was born from reckoning.

From the moment I stopped abandoning myself and began to ask what a structure might look like if it was built not from burnout, but from alignment.

The answers didn't come quickly. They arrived over time. Quietly. In lived moments. In reflection. In the courage to look again and again.

That's where LIFEWork Harmony™ began. Not as a framework. Not as a brand. As a question. *What would it mean to build something that doesn't break the people inside it?*

It is still unfolding. It listens. It adjusts. It holds.

It is now becoming the foundation of my next book, *Alignment*. A body of work shaped not by ambition, but by truth. It lives in rhythm, in relationship, in the structure that now supports the kind of clarity I once searched for outside myself.

A friend once gave me a plaque that sits quietly in my home. It reads:

'Life is a journey, not a destination.'

She was right. The crossings. The conversations. The quiet turning points. They are where we become.

This next part of the journey is a fork. One of many.

And if these pages have met you where you are, I would be honoured if you chose to walk the next part with me.

Once, I whispered *enough* in surrender.

But it wasn't the end.

It was the beginning of alignment.

ACKNOWLEDGEMENTS

To every person who helped me rise again, thank you.

Your presence, your patience, your truth, and your belief carried me through. Whether you offered guidance, laughter, silence or simple companionship, you became part of the reason I found my way back.

To my family, you held me without question.

To my friends, you spoke truth with love and stood with me through it all.

To the professionals, your care gave me space to breathe and strength to heal.

To every quiet moment that revealed clarity, truth, and direction, I see you now.

And to you, the reader, thank you for walking with me.

You did not just witness my story. You became part of it.

With deep appreciation,

Lorraine Travis

Continue the journey

To explore more of Lorraine's work, including her upcoming book Alignment, or to connect with LIFEWork Harmony™, visit:

https://balancepointsolutions.com.au

You are not alone on the path. Let this be the beginning of your next step.

My Soul Whispered, 'Enough'

www.ingramcontent.com/pod-product-compliance
Lightning Source LLC
Chambersburg PA
CBHW030329080526
44584CB00012B/771